Planning for Factory Automation

Other Books of Interest from McGraw-Hill

Ireson/Coombs
HANDBOOK OF RELIABILITY ENGINEERING AND MANAGEMENT

Kaewert/Frost
DEVELOPING EXPERT SYSTEMS FOR MANUFACTURING

Lubben
JUST-IN-TIME MANUFACTURING

Hodson
MAYNARD'S INDUSTRIAL ENGINEERING HANDBOOK

Nevins/Whitney
CONCURRENT DESIGN OF PRODUCTS AND PROCESSES

Stark
MANAGING CAD/CAM

Teicholz/Orr
COMPUTER INTEGRATED MANUFACTURING HANDBOOK

Cleland/Bidanda
THE AUTOMATED FACTORY HANDBOOK: TECHNOLOGY AND MANAGEMENT

Tompkins
WINNING MANUFACTURING

Feigenbaum
TOTAL QUALITY CONTROL

Juran
JURAN'S QUALITY CONTROL HANDBOOK

Slater
INTEGRATED PROCESS MANAGEMENT: A QUALITY MODEL

Taylor
OPTIMIZATION AND VARIATION REDUCTION IN QUALITY

Planning for Factory Automation

A Management Guide to World-Class Manufacturing

Peter G. Vanderspek, Ph.D.

McGraw-Hill, Inc.
New York   St. Louis   San Francisco   Auckland   Bogotá
Caracas   Lisbon   London   Madrid   Mexico   Milan
Montreal   New Delhi   Paris   San Juan   São Paulo
Singapore   Sydney   Tokyo   Toronto

Library of Congress Cataloging-in-Publication Data

Vanderspek, Peter G.
    Planning for factory automation : a management guide to world-class
    manufacturing / Peter G. Vanderspek.
        p.   cm.
    Includes index.
    ISBN 0-07-066949-X
    1. Production planning.   2. Automation.   3. Production management.
    I. Title.
    TS176.T33   1993
    658.5'14—dc20   92-16582
                                                                           CIP

1 2 3 4 5 6 7 8 9 0   DOC/DOC   9 8 7 6 5 4 3 2

ISBN 0-07-066949-X

*The sponsoring editor for this book was Gail F. Nalven, the editing supervisor was
Caroline Levine, and the production supervisor was Pamela A. Pelton. This book
was set in Baskerville by Carol Woolverton, Lexington, Mass., in cooperation with
Warren Publishing Services.*

Printed and bound by R. R. Donnelley & Sons Company.

*To my wife, Charlotte,
who encouraged and assisted me
in writing this book*

Contents

Foreword

This book is addressed especially to nontechnical general managers. It fills a need for a clearly written, readable introduction to a complex and often baffling topic. It also can serve well as a basic text or supplementary reading for business administration students who need to know about the growing importance of a sophisticated manufacturing sector.

Planning for Factory Automation provides an excellent, concise overview of what is involved in making U.S. manufacturers "world class" again. It will start top managers thinking of how to go about modernizing their organization as a whole as well as their manufacturing operations.

This book covers the major technologies and methodologies that must be adopted. It provides helpful guidelines for starting to plan the updating process, it outlines specific steps to be taken, and it lists pitfalls to be avoided in implementing the plan.

As we approach the twenty-first century, terms like total quality control, continuous improvement, participatory management, and factory automation are gaining recognition as essential ingredients for an economically successful country.

Several major corporations as well as numerous smaller companies have updated their organizations in an attempt to meet the serious competitive challenge from abroad that threatens to overwhelm them. However, for the United States to survive as a world-leading economy, the example of these companies must be followed by a majority of U.S. manufacturers. This book is intended to guide and inspire them to do so.

Robert E. Gulardo, I.E.
Vice President
The Benham Group

Preface

Time is running out for the United States to protect its position in the world economy as a first-class manufacturing power. Unless a majority of U.S. manufacturers of all sizes decide to quickly and effectively update their operations, the United States may well become a second-rate country with a reduced standard of living.

This book is intended to facilitate and promote the process of making U.S. manufacturing world class again by providing nontechnical as well as technical executives with a starting point and guide for modernizing their manufacturing enterprise.

Factory automation may appear to be an intimidating topic to many people who are not technically oriented. Factory automation is, in fact, a complex matter, beset by many problems and suffering from many misconceptions. One of the most damaging misconceptions is the notion that introducing factory automation is just a matter of installing a few pieces of highly sophisticated equipment.

This book goes to great lengths to show that effective planning for factory automation requires a complete overhaul of the entire manufacturing enterprise—not just automating the production process.

For this effort to be successful, all functions in the organization must be completely updated, and revolutionary changes must be made in management philosophy and in employee attitudes and relationships—from Chief Executive Officer on down.

Planning for Factory Automation attempts to clarify some of the basics involved in updating a manufacturing enterprise, eliminate some of the confusion and misconceptions in this area, and facilitate and promote the adoption of some of the new methodologies and technologies discussed in this book. It also guides the process of actually planning and implementing a sound updating program.

The first half of this book provides a comprehensive overview of the terminology, concepts, and components of an updating program. It covers the basic technologies and methodologies used and discusses the crucial role played by computers. It also deals with the concepts of flexible and cellular manufacturing, and with the application of these concepts in advanced manufacturing systems. It concludes with a brief review of the history and current status of automation and a look to the future.

This part of the book is directed mainly to the nontechnical executive who has had only limited exposure to factory automation and related topics. It also helps technical executives to discuss these matters with nontechnical executives.

The second half of this book deals with the dynamics of planning, including planning in general, the planning process for updating a manufacturing enterprise, the impact of an updating program on the plant building and the manufacturing process, changes needed in the human resources area, and justifying the expense of planning and implementing an updating program. Further, it discusses misconceptions and obstacles that tend to hinder progress, offers guidelines for facilitating the planning process, and reviews the need for outside assistance and the types of assistance available.

The challenge of updating the U.S. manufacturing sector is formidable but the task is doable. It is high time for America to face up to this challenge and rise to the occasion.

Acknowledgments

The author acknowledges his debt to the numerous automation experts who have advanced the state of the art by their articles and books on the subject of updating the manufacturing enterprise.

Special thanks to Richard H. France, MSAE, for his many valuable suggestions for improving the manuscript and to Charlie Branch for preparing the final text.

Peter G. Vanderspek
San Luis Obispo,
California

Planning for
Factory
Automation

1

Introduction

The Evolution of Manufacturing

In order to gain a perspective on the present state of U.S. manufacturing and to assess the need for updating the manufacturing enterprise, it is helpful to briefly review the various stages through which production technology has passed, and continues to pass, since the Industrial Revolution.

Focusing on the role played by people in the manufacturing process and on the types of tools they utilize, five stages can be distinguished:

1. *Manual.* People utilizing hand tools

2. *Mechanized.* Machines directly controlled by people

3. *Automated/mechanically driven.* Machines controlled by mechanical devices

4. *Automated/program driven.* Machines controlled by preprogrammed computers

5. *Computer-integrated manufacturing.* Machines controlled by a hierarchy of computers that direct the complete manufacturing process while guided by inputs from the various functional departments of the enterprise

The Industrial Revolution, which resulted in the second stage, made mass production and specialization possible. It also resulted in tremendous waste: physical, i.e., low-quality products, high scrappage, and high rework rates, as well as mental, i.e., craftsmen's skills were replaced by monotonous, routine tasks.

As manufacturing enters the fifth stage, most manual labor is likely to

1

be gradually eliminated, and all other direct human involvement in the manufacturing process will be substantially reduced. However, humans will still be needed in manufacturing, but in a more indirect manner. They will concentrate on idea conception, innovation, guidance, problem solving, and other tasks—mostly mental, rather than physical—for which humans still have an advantage over computer-driven machines.

The completely automated factory has become a feasible objective only recently as a result of very rapid progress in computer technology. The speed with which automation will spread depends to a large extent on three factors: (1) the development of more sophisticated and relatively low-cost automated equipment, (2) the successful integration of this equipment into a comprehensive production system, and, perhaps most important, (3) the presence of nontechnical conditions that favor, or at least do not hinder, such progress. The widespread application of comprehensive automation technology in the years ahead is expected to revolutionize the present manufacturing process and to have significant impacts on the economy and society in general.

The Past Four Decades

The origin of the difficult situation in which U.S. manufacturing finds itself at present can be traced to the early post-World War II period. At the end of the war, the United States was the undisputed, single, top manufacturing power in the world. The industrial base of practically all of its competitors had been destroyed or severely weakened as a result of the war. At the same time, pent-up domestic demand kept competitive pressures within the United States at a low level.

For a period of several decades, the United States continued to dominate its markets abroad, not only in market share but also in process engineering and productivity, while its imports of manufactured products were very limited. Production capacity was the key to profits, while cost and price were secondary.

The existence of this seller's market for such a long time brought about a number of changes in U.S. manufacturing that gradually began to cause serious problems:

- Little attention was paid to process innovation, except in semiconductors and a few other sectors.
- Quantity was emphasized at the expense of quality.

- Marketing and salesmanship were neglected.
- Bureaucracy in management proliferated.
- Inefficient factories continued to be operated, and few new ones were being built.
- Management's success was measured in short-term results, with little concern for the long term.
- Management became reactive and content to continue its mode of operations until forced to change by external circumstances.

Problems related to U.S. manufacturing competitiveness started to develop after the other major industrial economies began to gradually rebuild their manufacturing capability and incorporate newly developed technology. U.S. manufacturers by and large were slow in recognizing the handwriting on the wall and persisted in disregarding the rapidly rising competitiveness of Japan and western Europe.

By the early 1970s, the tide had completely turned: Many sectors of U.S. manufacturing had lost their competitive edge; U.S. exports had declined precipitously; and imports had soared, creating a sizable negative trade balance. Sectors that have been especially hard hit and have been all but lost to foreign competition include radios, basic metals, machine tools, shoes, appliances, clothing, cameras, textiles, and electronics.

In addition to the pervasive complacency that prevailed among most U.S. manufacturers until recently, there are several other factors that contributed to produce the present state of affairs.

During the past several decades, a fundamental change has taken place in the underlying basis for a country's competitive position, and thereby eventually its standard of living. Historically, the possession of valuable natural resources was a key factor in determining what a country produced and at what cost. Such resources include climate, minerals, metals, forests, agricultural land, fishing grounds, and location, especially proximity to waterways. However, in the 1960s, many countries began to focus their efforts on creating their own competitive advantage. By effectively utilizing new manufacturing technologies and adopting new management approaches, these countries were able to increase their productivity without the benefit of abundant natural resources.

Natural resources accounted for a major part of the previous prominence of the United States as a world leader in manufacturing. The successful efforts of other countries to compensate for their less favorable position in natural resources were bound to diminish the advantage of the United States—*unless* the United States made similar efforts, and this the United States has failed to do.

Another contributing factor was the slowdown in the rate of growth of U.S. manufacturing capacity in the early 1970s. This reduced the opportunity to incorporate new technology when adding new capacity and created, therefore, a need for justifying investments in new technology in existing installations—an added obstacle to the introduction of such technology.

Especially alarming from a more general economic point of view are the low rates of saving and investment in the United States and the lackluster performance of the U.S. educational system, particularly in the hard sciences and engineering, in comparison with Japan and other industrial countries.

After painting this somewhat dismal picture of the present state of U.S. manufacturing, it is appropriate to highlight some of its continuing strengths:

- Overall, U.S. manufacturing is still the most productive in the world, with Japan only recently coming close to the United States.

- U.S. manufacturing continues to increase its productivity, albeit at a much slower rate than several major competitors.

- U.S. manufacturing continues to account for about 22 percent of the country's gross national product, even while employment in manufacturing continues to decline.

- Most of the automation technologies and new approaches to management that have been developed thus far originated in the United States; nevertheless, the United States is lagging badly in applying this technology and these new approaches to its own manufacturing sector.

However, these strengths will not save the United States from falling behind its major competitors abroad. If the overall economic performance of the United States and of its major competitors were to continue at the same relative rates as at present, U.S. overall productivity—and thus the U.S. standard of living—would drop below those of Japan and several countries in Europe within the next 20 years.

Such an assumption is likely to be at best only partially correct since widely divergent growth rates rarely continue for a long period of time. Nevertheless, the situation is serious enough for the United States to make a sustained all-out effort to upgrade its economic performance, especially as regards its manufacturing sector.

Automation Abroad

Since foreign competition in manufactured products is one of the main forces driving the process of updating the U.S. manufacturing sector, it is helpful to briefly review what has been happening abroad, especially as regards robotics.

Although the United States started as the world's leader in machine tools and pioneered the development of robots, the United States currently trails well behind Japan in applying automation technology—especially robotics—to the manufacturing sector. Japan has produced and installed a far larger number of robots than any other country and is trying hard to outdistance the United States in developing new robot technology also. The United States may still be number one in computers and robotic controls, but its lead is being eroded rapidly.

Utilizing robot and related technology developed in the United States, Japan launched the robot revolution in manufacturing in 1967. The reasons why Japan had, and still has, a greater interest in robots than the United States include: a heavy emphasis on quality, a shrinking labor supply, a high concern for productivity, a cooperative relationship between labor and management, and government encouragement and support. As is the case in the United States, the automobile industry in Japan absorbed the largest number of robots, followed by the electronics industry.

Japan has been concentrating on installing large numbers of non-sophisticated robots, including devices not considered to be true robots in the United States. Also, Japan has been relatively weak in developing the software required to operate the robots. However, both these conditions are changing rapidly, and Japan is now also taking the lead in producing very advanced robots and is strengthening its capability to develop software. Thus, it is expected that Japan will remain the world's number one producer and exporter of all types of robots for the foreseeable future.

Less clear at this time is Japan's future role in developing the completely automated factory that requires the integration of various components of the automated production process as well as the adoption by top management of a completely new approach to manufacturing and operating a business. It is true that Japan has made an excellent start by installing a larger number of so-called flexible automated manufacturing systems than have been installed in the United States and western Europe. Also, several years ago, Japan constructed the world's first almost completely automated factory. Even so, it is not certain that Japan will be able to dominate the factory automation market, especially since several giant U.S. companies, such as IBM, General Electric, and Westinghouse, entered the picture several years ago.

Several countries in Europe also have made progress in factory automation. Germany ranks third in robot usage, behind Japan and the United States. Other countries with significant involvement in automation include Sweden, the United Kingdom, France, Italy, and Norway.

The Challenge Today

It appears that the topic of factory automation is of considerable general interest to manufacturers in this country. However, many chief executive officers and general managers are not prepared to deal effectively with the question of whether, when, how, and to what extent their manufacturing operation should be updated by the introduction of totally new methodology and equipment.

Although a number of U.S. manufacturers have begun to realize that they have serious problems that cannot be solved by stopgap measures or by government assistance in the foreign trade area, many manufacturers have not yet accepted the fact that, unless they initiate a comprehensive, well-planned program for change, they are likely to be forced out of business in a relatively short period of time.

Some manufacturers demand government action in the form of higher tariffs or import quotas. A large number of manufacturers still are sitting on the fence, waiting and hoping that somehow their problems will fade away in due time. Only a modest number have taken the necessary step of deciding to update their operation to be able to meet global competition. This attitude in the United States contrasts sharply with that prevailing in Japan and several countries in western Europe, where significantly more progress has been made in making the manufacturing sector more competitive.

Lack of understanding and misconceptions about the applicability of automation, fear of the widespread impact of the new technology on the whole enterprise, and concern about the financial requirements for implementing a drastic overhaul are some of the most common reasons why action often is postponed. Top management in the United States tends to be reluctant to accept risk and emphasizes short-term profitability at the expense of pursuing long-term, strategic benefits.

Manufacturing is likely to remain a sizable sector of the U.S. economy only if a sufficiently large number of U.S. manufacturers decide to do what is required to raise productivity, lower their costs, and satisfy the changing demands of today's worldwide marketplace. The failure, thus far, of many U.S. manufacturers to respond effectively to the challenge they face and make the necessary investment of time, effort, and money is a serious problem for the United States.

A massive infusion of new automation technology and—even more important—a virtual revolution in managing a manufacturing enterprise is required to reverse the decline of U.S. competitiveness in the manufacturing sector. Unfortunately, the outlook for a significant acceleration in updating efforts is not encouraging. Investments of the type required have been modest and may not soon reach the level needed to revitalize U.S. manufacturing.

Some of the reasons for this disappointing current and anticipated performance are reviewed in this book. However, the main focus of this planning guide is to assist U.S. manufacturing management in facing up to their problem and in planning a custom-made program that will help them restore the competitiveness and long-term viability of their enterprises.

2

Automation Equipment

Factory automation and updating are elusive concepts. They encompass a large variety of new types of equipment and new approaches to manufacturing that have been developed over the past several decades and continue to be developed, and that are being applied in a variety of configurations and environments.

The number of new, technically intricate components and concepts that are related to factory automation is almost limitless. A voluminous new nomenclature has evolved that tries to cover the expanding array of automation technology.

In this chapter five major types of equipment are reviewed that are utilized in an automated factory: machine tools, industrial robots, materials-handling equipment, sensing technologies, and data collection technologies. Computers and software programs are covered separately in Chap. 3.

Although the discussion is slanted toward the fabrication and assembly of metal products, most of it is also applicable to most other manufacturing sectors.

Machine Tools

Computerized numerically controlled machine tools constitute the most basic element of most automated manufacturing installations. They have evolved from manual operation via punched cards or tape to autonomous control by a single dedicated computer. At present the operations of several machine tools can be jointly controlled and coordinated by a hierarchy of computers as part of a comprehensive, integrated manufacturing program.

Computer-controlled machine tools for turning and machining continue to gain in sophistication. They are becoming more flexible, more accurate, more reliable, i.e., higher uptime, and more intelligent. They may combine both milling and turning functions, they require less setup time, and they have faster feeds and spindle speeds and overall shorter cycle times.

Notable special features on computer-controlled machine tools can include automatic tool cribs and automatic tool-changing systems; tool monitoring and sensing (to check on tool wear and breakage); automatic in-process and postprocess gaging and touch trigger probing of the workpiece (to control and adjust the machining process); multiple spindles (to be able to perform several tasks with a single setup); and up to five axes (including swivel spindles, tilt tables, and pallet index).

An automated machine tool can be upgraded into a machining center by incorporating a robot for tool changing and workpiece handling. Such machining centers can be linked with other types of automated equipment to form an integrated manufacturing system as discussed in Chap. 5.

Industrial Robots

After the original introduction of robots several decades ago, expectations were high that robots would rapidly begin to play a crucial role in manufacturing, with sales anticipated at several billion dollars by 1990. As it turned out, these expectations were totally unrealistic. After peaking in 1984 to 1985, robot sales collapsed and sales volume has since continued to increase at only a modest rate.

One of the reasons for the early problems with robots was that the available software seriously lagged behind the robot's mechanical capabilities. Basically, it was not realized that a typical manufacturing operation cannot properly utilize and interface with such a totally new type of equipment without considerable modification and accommodation of the overall system.

As a result, robots were installed in some plants without giving much thought as to how the robots would interface with the other components of the operation. Many were installed simply as laborsaving devices and in applications for which they were not cost-effective. Also, a major change in a plant's production process often eliminated the original, limited use of a robot, and the robot would end up standing idle.

Robot manufacturers also are to blame for the early problems. The manufacturers tended to design and market robots without paying much attention as to how their products were going to fit into the overall manufacturing process, and they offered little or no after-the-sale service. As a result, the robot industry experienced a difficult time with shakeouts and takeovers during which expansion was limited and little or no profit was made.

More recently, however, the industrial robot is finally beginning to come into its own and is gradually being accepted as a vital component of automated manufacturing systems. Robot manufacturers have begun to better understand and to cater to their customers' needs, and some are now primary participants in the overall automation installation process, either by also manufacturing other components or aligning themselves with manufacturers of such components.

Even so, robotics has a long way to go before its full potential is realized. Perhaps no more than 1 out of every 10 manufacturing enterprises that could profitably use a robot actually has one.

Robots add a totally new dimension to the manufacturing process. A robot can be defined simply as a reprogrammable multipurpose manipulator of varying degrees of sophistication, intelligence, and flexibility.

In essence, robots can do some of the tasks that could previously be performed only by human labor, but with several notable differences. Even the most sophisticated robot today is far less flexible in its capabilities than a human worker. On the other hand, robots can do certain tasks with greater consistent precision and for much longer periods of time than human workers can. In fact, robots can perform certain tasks that humans are unable to do, e.g., those in microassembly and in inhospitable environments.

Robots should be considered as only one possible component of an automated manufacturing installation. They are usually not the principal component, and their usefulness typically depends on how effectively and appropriately they are integrated into the overall operation.

A large variety of robots has been developed for different applications, requiring different capabilities and different degrees of sophistication. Industrial robots can be used for such tasks as arc and spot welding, die casting, spray painting, materials handling (including as an adjunct to a machine tool), and assembly. Typical materials-handling tasks for which robots are suitable include palletizing and depalletizing, bin picking and kitting, sorting, loading of machine tools, and case packing.

Robots can be especially effective if they are used for repetitive tasks, for handling awkward parts, in hazardous environments, when multiple shifts are needed, when the manual operation generates a lot of scrap due to lack of sufficient accuracy, and when the parts are very small and require precise tolerances.

At present most robots still are used only for simple, routine tasks, including pick-and-place operations. Welding still accounts for the highest percentage of robot use.

The use of robots in assembly—one of their most sophisticated applications—is limited by the fact that most products are not specifically designed for assembly by robots. The topic Design for Assembly (DFA) is discussed in Concurrent Engineering in Chap. 4. As DFA becomes implemented in the years ahead, robots are likely to be used much more extensively in assembly work.

Assembly is a task which especially utilizes one of the most outstanding characteristics of robots, i.e., their flexibility. They can be made to assemble an almost limitless variety of products. In most assembly tasks, high accuracy and consistency are also essential requirements.

Normally, a robot must be "taught," i.e., programmed, step by step how to assemble the parts. However, newer software programs are decreasing the complexity of programming. In fact, a software program is reported to have been developed that can make it possible for a robot to teach itself by trial and error how to properly assemble the various component parts of a product; the resulting assembly instructions can then be used by other robots in the regular assembly process.

Some of the problems of using robots are difficulty of programming, the high cost of software, unreliable peripherals—i.e., tooling, fixturing, parts presentation, etc.—programming languages that differ from one robot brand to another, and difficulty in integrating robots with other automated equipment. These problems are gradually being overcome. Programming is becoming simpler and can often be done off line. Progress is being made in making different brands of robots more compatible. Vendors are becoming more service oriented and are beginning to offer, for example, fully integrated robotic assembly systems.

The basic cost of a robot ranges between $25,000 and $100,000, depending on its sophistication. To this must be added the cost of accessories (such as end effectors that often must be customer designed, e.g., to pick up specific parts), installation, and integration. The total cost of a robot installation is likely to run between three and six times the cost of the basic robot. Planning such a system may take from 6 to 12 months.

The cost of peripheral equipment will vary according to the type of robot. For an assembly robot, peripherals may add up to 300 percent to the cost of the robot; for an arc-welding robot, up to 100 percent; for a spot-welding robot, 33 percent; and for a spray-painting robot, up to 45 percent. In the case of an assembly robot, the equipment required to feed parts to the robot will typically account for at least half the cost of the total system, while software may constitute from 10 to 35 percent.

A robot's usual work life is up to 10 years, but some may last longer. Many robots—especially six-axis articulated robots—can be switched from one type of basic function to another by reprogramming and retooling them, as long as they have the required "reach," i.e., configuration, and payload capacity.

Such switching is cost-effective in many cases since the original cost of the robot is generally paid for within the usual 2- or 3-year depreciation cycle and the cost of modifying the robot for a new task is often much less than the cost of a new robot. Typical exceptions may include switching to assembly, spot welding, or arc welding, where vision guidance and/or the cost of retooling may be prohibitive.

It is advisable, therefore, when buying a robot for a specific function, to try to anticipate other possible future uses and consider buying a high-quality robot of a slightly bigger size than needed. Also, make sure that more sensors can be added if they are needed later. However, if a vision-guidance requirement is anticipated, this capability might be better incorporated in the original robot since vision tends to be much cheaper if it is built in than when it is added later.

Anticipated refinements in robot capabilities over the next several years include multiple arms, improved end effectors ("hands"), mobility (moving on tracks or even without tracks), considerably higher accuracy, easier and more off-line programming, and better vision and other sensory perception.

Materials-Handling Equipment

Until rather recently, the importance of the materials-handling function in manufacturing was largely overlooked. It was only when the manufacturing process was carefully scrutinized for possibilities to cut more than just labor cost, that it became apparent that materials handling was one of the key areas for further upgrading the manufacturing operation.

In many production facilities, materials spend as much as 85 to 95 percent of the time either waiting to be worked on or being moved. Also, materials handling often takes up more than half of the floor space of a factory.

It is not surprising, therefore, that storage and handling account for as much as 75 percent of a product's total manufacturing and distribution cost. This, in turn, means that a significant improvement in materials-handling efficiency is vital to achieve the optimum benefits of updating a manufacturing installation.

Automated materials-handling systems provide the essential physical link for combining isolated automated manufacturing processes into a comprehensive, integrated system. In addition, a highly efficient automated materials-handling system is of crucial importance when introducing the just-in-time approach to manufacturing, which is discussed in Chap. 4.

To be effective, automated materials-handling systems must be fully compatible and integrated with factory information and control systems. They should also be modular so they can be rearranged and/or expanded when necessary.

Another requirement is that they are sufficiently flexible, e.g., to allow for different loads, speeds, or sizes. Since manufacturing has to become more flexible to be able to respond to the increasing demand for a higher variety and lower volume of each type of product, materials-handling systems will also have to become more flexible and, as a result, more complex.

Most types of materials-handling equipment have been in existence—in at least some basic form—for several decades. Hardware technology appears to have just about reached maturity. New applications and higher capabilities mostly depend on expanding and modifying existing hardware, combined with constantly improving the controls and software.

There are at least three problem areas in automated materials-handling systems. The first problem is interfacing with the various other systems of an automated factory: More glitches are likely, particularly during the start-up period, when there are a large number of interfaces. To minimize this type of problem, it is best to start utilizing a new, automated materials-handling system at a rate well below its optimum capacity and gradually increase the rate over the first 12 to 18 months of operation.

The enormous complexity of the required software to operate such a system is a second source of problems, especially because of the need to provide for compatible communication among the various computer-controlled systems. The third area concerns the synchronization of the various elements of each system. Careful planning is needed to ensure that each component is fully developed and available to be integrated with every other component of the system.

As discussed in the previous section, robots are already playing an active role in materials handling, and this role is expected to expand significantly over the years ahead. Three other types of automated materials-handling equipment that are finding increased application in today's updated manufacturing plants are reviewed below: automated guided vehicles, automated conveyors, and automated storage and retrieval systems.

Automated Guided Vehicles

Automated Guided Vehicles (AGVs) have been called an offspring of the towline as well as a hybrid of a forklift truck and a conveyor. However, today's AGV is a unique piece of materials-handling equipment that can be defined as a driverless, battery-powered, electronically guided vehicle that is available in a wide variety of types and applications. They are extremely versatile and are becoming increasingly sophisticated.

Many AGVs are still used as towing vehicles to move a large volume of heavy materials, e.g., from storage to factory floor. However, other types of AGVs are tailor-made for automated factories that require flexibility and just-in-time materials handling.

AGVs include unit-load vehicles that operate alone and carry a single pallet as well as light-load vehicles that carry containers with small parts and components. An AGV equipped with movable forks is used in automated factories to move palletized materials at different levels from one location to another.

An AGV can also be used as an assembly line vehicle, transporting subassemblies to the assembly line. When equipped with a robot on board, an AGV can function in such capacities as a moving assembly platform, a machine tool-loading and -unloading system, and a traveling tool holder. Special features that make AGVs useful for a variety of tasks include several types of load transfer decks and scissor-type lifts for self-loading and unloading.

Load capacities vary widely and can be as high as 120,000 pounds. Speeds typically range between 40 and 200 feet per minute. Batteries usually must be recharged after about 8 hours of use. The normal service life of an AGV is 15 to 20 years.

Guidance for AGVs can be provided in various ways. The oldest and still most common type of guidance system employs a wire guide path embedded in the factory floor. The wire is energized from the central control station and is then "sensed" by the vehicle for guidance. This wire also carries information that is picked up via the AGV's antenna.

Advantages of this system include that it works well even in fairly dirty environments and heavy traffic, and is free from outside interference. However, it is inflexible, and it is costly and time-consuming to repair and alter the wire path.

A second major system uses a painted guide path. Photo sensors aboard the AGV pick up reflected light and activate the steering mechanism. A more sophisticated version uses ultraviolet light on the AGV to stimulate chemical particles in the painted path that then generate visible light; a sensor on the vehicle sees and tracks this light. The path contains information codes at various points to control the movement of the AGV. Variations of the painted path system include a plastic strip containing fluorescent particles as well as metallic tape, in which case metal-sensing technology is used.

Advantages of the painted path and plastic strip include that they can be applied to a wide variety of flooring materials (even some carpets) and that the path can be changed quickly, i.e., repainting or retaping takes only a few hours. Disadvantages of the painted path and the plastic strip include that they do not work well on dirty floors and that they must be repainted or retaped frequently. Also, to be flexible, these two methods require a separate radio communications system for relaying instructions from a stationary controlling computer.

The most recently developed guidance systems operate without any fixed guide paths, i.e., they do not depend on any embedded wires, painted lines, strips, or tapes. One such self-guided vehicle utilizes an on-board dead-reckoning system which measures wheel rotation and steer angle. To correct for wheel slippage and other causes of inaccuracy, a second on-board system obtains locational information at various points along the path, e.g., by means of a scanning laser beam that reads bar-code targets on the wall. Other self-guided systems are based on infrared triangulation, on inertial guidance using sonar sensors and gyroscopes, or on ultrasonic systems.

AGVs are continually becoming more sophisticated, with more on-board computer intelligence and greater guidance control capabilities, including radio frequency communication, laser optics, infrared links, and bar-code location identification. Also, more of these vehicles will feature vision capability for even greater tracking accuracy.

In addition, an increasing number of AGVs will be equipped with a robot on board, and the controls of these two types of equipment will be better integrated. This will enable AGVs to be used as links between so-called islands of automation without human intervention.

Over the years ahead, an ever larger variety of vehicles are expected to become available, especially light-load vehicles. AGVs will become more reliable and, as a result of standardization, probably more affordable.

Automated Conveyors

In addition to AGVs, there are a number of other automated transportation systems for use within a manufacturing installation. Unlike the newer types of AGVs, these other systems all depend on physical paths for their operation.

Mostly known as conveyors, they can be either floor mounted or overhead mounted. Floor-mounted conveyors are an old standby of materials handling. They are powered by means of a chain, rollers, or a belt, and are used in a wide variety of applications. They are efficient and relatively low in cost, but take up valuable floor space and limit access to other equipment.

Overhead-mounted conveyors include the already well-established Power-and-Free (P&F) conveyor system and the more recently introduced Automated Electrified Monorail (AEM) system.

P&F systems employ two tracks: a drive track with a continuous chaindrive and a second, separate track that supports the carriers. The carriers can be disengaged from the drive track to control their movement as instructed by a computer.

P&F systems provide effective high-volume nonsynchronous handling of all types of materials. They are relatively cheap and are simple to operate and maintain. However, they are subject to a lot of wear and tear, and are difficult to expand.

The AEM is a sophisticated version of the much older nonelectrified automated monorail. In the latter system, trolleys are uniformly pulled along a fixed path. In an AEM, by contrast, each trolley is independently motorized and is controlled by a computer via the electrical bus bar on the rail; it moves only when instructed, changes speed as needed, and travels to various locations as directed.

AEMs can be used as a buffer storage system, as a system for just-in-time delivery of parts and components to the assembly process, and as a conveyor of workpieces within the assembly operation. Depending on their use, they can be mounted at various heights above the floor; also, an inverted version is available that is mounted on the floor.

The trolleys of an AEM can carry heavy loads, up to 10,000 pounds each, and can run at speeds of up to 600 feet per minute. Since AEM systems are modular, they can be relatively easily expanded and modified. AEMs have become especially entrenched in the automotive industry, but they are also gaining a foothold in other manufacturing sectors.

AEMs have several advantages over P&F systems, including higher speed, higher positioning accuracy, on-board power for lifting and other devices, ability to reverse their direction, and on-board intelligence. However, AEMs are several times more costly than P&F systems.

Both AEMs and P&F systems tend to be more cost-effective than the much more expensive AGV system in cases where a large number of units must be transported quickly, especially when space is limited and a high level of flexibility is not of prime importance.

Automated Storage and Retrieval Systems

Automated Storage and Retrieval Systems (AS/RSs) are widely used in both manufacturing and warehousing. They can be described as computer-controlled systems that can move materials into and out of high-density storage areas and record all related information with little or no human intervention.

A typical AS/RS consists of three major components: a storage structure, one or more Storage/Retrieval (S/R) machines, and a control system. Other components include pickup and delivery stations, conveyors, pallets or containers, and fire-protection systems.

The storage structure, made up of racks, can be built inside a conventional, free-standing building, or it can be constructed without a separate building envelope by adding sides and a roof to the rack structure. In the latter configuration, the facility is known as a "rack supported building." Most AS/RS buildings are rather tall in order to conserve space and attain the high storage density that is a major advantage of the AS/RS. Storage spaces in the racks are usually of uniform size and load capacity.

Each automated S/R machine, or stacker crane, travels on rails in a narrow aisle. It may have one or two masts, is equipped with position sensors, and is capable of moving loads to and from any location in the racks on either side of the aisle, as instructed by the controlling computer.

The control system may include several computers (minicomputers, microcomputers, and/or programmable logic controllers). The system may control one or several S/R machines. A complex system can integrate various functions, including receiving, storage, packing, and shipping.

AS/RSs are being used more and more for materials handling as well as storage and retrieval. They can handle loads of up to thousands of pounds of raw materials, work in process, finished products, fixtures, tooling, and pallets.

AS/RSs were originally designed to handle unit loads on pallets and were constructed in increasingly larger sizes. One structure boasted a record 120 aisles. However, as the trend toward reducing inventories became stronger during the past several years—in accordance with the just-in-time approach—there has been a corresponding shift from large unit-load AS/RSs to smaller systems that may also be used for staging, routing, and in-storage buffering. Simultaneously, demand has grown for completely different types of AS/RSs, especially on the part of manufacturing operations.

One such different type of AS/RS is the miniload system. Instead of pallets, it usually handles containers or trays ("totes")—often subdivided into compartments of different sizes—that contain small items. The totes are captive to the system and carry loads that usually weigh less than 500 pounds.

Specific totes are retrieved from their storage locations, as directed by the computer system, and delivered by an unstaffed, aisle-captive automated S/R machine to end-of-aisle picking stations for computer-directed manual picking by operators. Alternatively, totes can be delivered to so-called pickup and dropoff stations that directly shuttle the retrieved loads to conveyors or other equipment for delivery elsewhere in the plant. For a storage operation, the same sequence is generally followed in reverse.

Miniload AS/RSs can also be used to directly support manufacturing work cells if such cells are located along the outer perimeter of a miniload rack structure. They can provide parts, etc., directly to the cells through peripheral openings in the racks.

Miniload AS/RSs are faster and more versatile than unit-load AS/RSs and are ideally suited for multiuse applications in flexible automated manufacturing operations. In many cases, a unit-load system will still be required, in addition to one or more miniload systems, to handle heavy, bulky items.

Another type of AS/RS that is somewhat comparable in function to the miniload AS/RS is the automated carousel S/R system. In this system, all stored totes filled with small items move simultaneously in carousel fashion, either horizontally or vertically, past an automated movable extractor mechanism controlled by a stationary S/R machine that places selected totes on a belt for delivery to one or more workstations. At the workstation, an operator picks the parts that are needed for kitting, spares, etc. It is anticipated that parts picking from totes, whether in miniload systems or carousel systems, will eventually be handled by robots that are specially programmed for such tasks.

AS/RSs offer many advantages over nonautomated systems: they require less space and fewer workers; they reduce product damage and pilferage; they result in more accurate inventory management and control; and they provide easy accessibility of all items at all levels of a storage system and faster and more reliable delivery. The two main disadvantages of AS/RSs are the difficulty of modifying and expanding the system, especially unit-load systems, and their high capital cost. A typical unit-load system costs several million dollars.

AS/RSs can be made to directly interface with other components of the materials-handling system—including AGVs, robots, AEMs, etc.—to form a completely integrated system for storage and handling. In fact, only such an integrated system will fully optimize the benefits of an AS/RS and maximize the system's cost effectiveness.

Further refinements of AS/RSs are likely to be concentrated in control and software, including, for example, the spread of infrared and laser optical communications between computers on S/R machines and stationary controlling computers. These refinements will result in still more precise positioning and faster speeds of S/R machines, shorter cycle times, and higher throughput. Also, modular design AS/RSs are becoming more popular, and this is likely to bring down the high cost of these systems.

Sensing Technologies

Automated sensing devices provide an essential link in an automated manufacturing installation by collecting raw data from the manufacturing process. When combined with computer power, they can perform a large variety of functions, including identification, inspection, monitoring, maintaining inventories, and control.

The simplest automated sensing function is the identification of specially coded items, e.g., marking them with a bar code. This topic is covered in the next section, "Data Collection Technologies."

Generally speaking, the higher the degree of automation, the greater the need for more and better automated sensing, including higher accuracy, faster delivery, more intelligent manipulation of the collected data, and quicker utilization of this information.

There are a large variety of both contact- and noncontact-sensing devices that find application in automated manufacturing installations. They include simple electromechanical limit switches, proximity switches (based on magnetics), ultrasonic sensors (a primitive sonar), microwave sensors, laser sensors, torque sensors, tactile sensors, and sophisticated machine vision systems that are comparable to, and more accurate than, the human eye.

When machine vision was first introduced in the 1960s, the technology was oversold, misunderstood, and misapplied. As a result, machine vision suffered a setback that lasted for about two decades. In recent years, however, the technology has finally come into its own and is now being accepted as a valuable component of automated manufacturing systems that can be very cost-effective in certain applications.

A machine vision system consists of a camera, controller, interface circuitry, and display terminal. The system is a noncontact device that can scan an entire object at once, determine patterns, and discern subtle details. It is typically used on line and can inspect 100 percent of the items being processed. Overall, it has greater capabilities than most other sensing devices.

Over the past decade or so, machine vision technology has made rapid progress. The user interface has become much friendlier, and operating the system no longer requires a highly skilled computer programmer. Minicomputers have been replaced by much cheaper personal computers. The system also has become more tolerant of fluctuations in lighting, reflections, and other interferences that originally limited its use on the plant floor.

Although the cost of a machine vision system has dropped considerably, it still is the most expensive sensing device because of its complexity and its need for extensive computer power. This makes it cost-effective only in cases where a simpler sensing device would not suffice.

Machine vision systems have found wide application in automated manufacturing installations. They are used, for example, to enhance the capability of robots, upgrade materials-handling equipment, improve the operation of machine tools, and provide input for statistical quality control programs. Specific functions typically performed by machine vision systems include: inspection, monitoring, positioning, sorting, and control.

A vision system is especially appropriate for on-line, 100 percent *inspection* in a high-speed manufacturing process. The system can be "trained" to recognize colors, shape, size, etc., and can be made to reject or signal defective items. Specific tasks include: assembly inspection (part presence and alignment), part inspection (measurement and defects), and packaging inspection (closure, fill-level, and label).

The *monitoring* function includes checking and measuring automated processes to ensure that standards are met and to warn of any deviations that might require human intervention before product defects begin to occur.

A machine vision system can be used for precise *positioning* of carts, pallets, and parts, and for *sorting* parts based on shape. They can also be used in a feedback *control* capacity to guide the operation of robots, machine tools, and other automated equipment.

There is one other technology that should be noted in connection with machine vision. Although not a vision system as such, digital imaging is a technique that can be used for enhancing an image so it can be seen more clearly by humans and so that it becomes easier to extract certain features. By applying a computer software program, false color can be added to show temperature ranges, edges can be made sharper, and contrast can be increased or decreased.

By combining digital imaging with X-rays or infrared rays or ultraviolet rays, it becomes possible to see images and features that would otherwise be invisible to the human eye. Digital imaging is used in high-value applications. At present its use is limited mostly to the medical field and the military, but it is expected to find increasing application in automated manufacturing.

Besides being useful as a technique for enhancing an image, digital imaging also can be used to transform information in any form—including handwritten or typed notes and various computer text formats as well as pictures and maps—into digital form. By digitizing all information, digital imaging could be used to eliminate the use of paper for storing and viewing information of all types in every department of a manufacturing enterprise. When implemented to its fullest extent, this would result in a "paperless" company.

It is expected that the use of automated sensing devices—and especially of machine vision systems—will increase significantly over the years ahead. Sensors are becoming "smarter" and are being integrated more and more by the original manufacturers with the equipment they serve, rather than being added later by the user. True three-dimensional vision is gradually becoming a reality. The number of sensors per robot will continue to increase, and this will make robots substantially more capable and flexible than at present.

Data Collection Technologies

Accurate and timely information is the lifeblood of an updated manufacturing enterprise. Manual data-collection methods such as handwriting and keyboarding do not fulfill the need for high speed and a high degree of accuracy. As a result, sophisticated data-collection technologies are beginning to be utilized that allow automated equipment to function at optimum effectiveness.

There is a basic need for each item in the manufacturing process to be identified as it moves from one location to another. Such information is accumulated and stored in computer memory, and is used in making decisions concerning the processing and handling of each item. Items to be identified and tracked include raw materials, parts, work in process, finished products, tools, fixtures, pallets, containers, etc.

Several technologies are available to identify items automatically, a process known as Automatic Identification (Auto.ID). The most widely used Auto.ID technology in manufacturing is bar coding. Bar coding is still not in universal use in manufacturing; it is used mostly in shipping and inventory control, but gains are being made in applying it in the actual production process.

A bar code consists of dark bars of different widths separated by light spaces that represent numbers, letters, and/or symbols. The bar code is decoded by an optical scanner that transforms the reflected optical pattern into electrical signals that, in turn, are transmitted to a computer. The light source used for optical scanning is a laser or light-emitting diode.

The bar code on the item is initially produced by some type of bar-code printer. Printing techniques have advanced from impact dot matrix to thermal printing and then to thermal transfer printing. The latter is currently the most effective method. It allows very high speeds, can use a wide range of label materials on which to print the code, and can be used in a high-temperature environment—all important factors to be considered for plant floor applications. Instead of acquiring a bar-code printer, it can sometimes be advantageous to purchase preprinted bar-code labels.

Another device for producing bar codes is the computer-controlled ink jet printer. This system allows the printing of bar codes directly onto, for example, shipping containers without using a separate label.

Scanning equipment can be either hand-held or stationary; a hand-held scanner can also be placed in a fixed-position stand for dual use. Hand-held scanners can be either of a contact or noncontact type.

There are three types of fixed-mount scanners: line, raster, and omnidirectional. The latter type of scanner, even though it is the most expensive, is especially appropriate for use in manufacturing because it allows scanning of items that are not positioned uniformly. All of these options should be investigated to ensure that a system will be selected that best fits the individual requirements of each company.

Since the collected information is intended to be used also outside the manufacturing enterprise, e.g., by suppliers of raw materials, parts, and components, and by distributors of the finished product, the code symbology must be the same for all parties involved. At present five symbologies have become generally accepted as standard and are being utilized by various industries.

These symbologies cover the formation of characters and strings of characters in bar codes. A key part of the bar code is the data identifier—the first few characters that indicate what type of item is being identified, e.g., a part, a product, a manufacturer, etc.

Bar coding has several advantages over other Auto.ID technologies, as well as a major drawback. Low cost is its main advantage: Bar-code labels are extremely inexpensive, and preprinted labels can be purchased at reasonable cost. Other advantages are the availability of off-the-shelf software, a high degree of accuracy in many applications, simple installation, and easy training of operators in using the technology. The major disadvantage of bar coding is its susceptibility to hostile and dirty environmental conditions, such as very high or low temperatures, grease, oil, paint, and other substances that affect the legibility of the code.

The next most commonly used Auto.ID technology in manufacturing is Radio Frequency Identification (RFID). It consists of "readers" and "tags" (transponders). The reader includes an antenna for transmitting and receiving signals from each tag, a microprocessor, and other electronics.

The tag includes an antenna, control logic, memory, and electronics for sending and receiving. A tag that contains a battery to power some or all of its functions is called an active tag. A passive tag does not have a battery and uses a portion of the power it receives from the reader to perform all of its functions.

Read-only tags are programmed by their manufacturer and cannot be reprogrammed. Read/write tags can be programmed with information in the location in which they operate. The capacity of tags varies widely and can range up to 512 bits of information; an even more sophisticated tag is in effect a portable data base and can carry information in text form. If a tag has information-processing capability—usually achieved by adding a microprocessor—it is known as an "intelligent tag."

At present, all RFID systems are closed, i.e., their tags can be read only by readers in their own company. Most RFID systems use low-frequency bidirectional radio signals. When a reader approaches a tag, the reader's signals on a specific frequency instruct the tag to transmit its message to the reader. If the tag has read/write capability, its message can be updated by the reader.

RFID systems have several advantages over bar coding: They can operate without a line of direct sight, are not impaired by harsh environments, can handle a larger amount of data, offer more flexibility, are more accurate, and can operate at longer distances.

Disadvantages of RFID systems include their much higher cost and the lack of standards that would make the systems of manufacturers compatible with those of their suppliers and distributors. It is expected that RFID will continue to be limited mostly to applications where bar coding is not feasible—until such time as its cost will drop and standards will be adopted.

In addition to bar coding and RFID, there are a number of other Auto.ID technologies that have had only limited application to manufacturing thus far. They include optical-character recognition and voice-data entry.

Optical-character recognition is somewhat similar to a bar coding system, except that stylized letters and numerals are printed and scanned instead of bar codes. Its use in manufacturing is expected to advance at a very modest pace.

Voice-data entry has had some success in office applications but has not made much headway on the factory floor, partly because of the problem of interference from background noise. The technology has not matured yet and is presently useful mainly as a complementary method for entering data. Voice-data entry is especially useful in applications where the information consists of words rather than numbers and where the operator's hands must be free to manipulate, e.g., an item to be inspected.

In addition to the various technologies described, a complementary technology known as Radio Frequency Data Communication (RFDC) is available. This technology is used to transmit the data collected by computer terminals by means of Auto.ID devices to a distant central computer.

RFDC greatly facilitates the speedy, real-time transmission of such data between distant locations. Installation requires careful planning to minimize the radio interference caused by the various buildings that are included in the system.

Auto.ID technologies are an essential ingredient of any comprehensive updating program. However, they can be installed in a manufacturing enterprise even if no further updating or automation is contemplated.

Auto.ID is becoming increasingly sophisticated. Its use in manufacturing is spreading rapidly as an excellent means of improving productivity and control while decreasing in-process inventories. It has a typical payback of less than a year and a half. Bar coding, in particular, is a cost-effective technology that is relatively easy to implement, even in a small manufacturing enterprise.

3
Computers and Software

This chapter includes a discussion of the vital role played by computers in an updated manufacturing enterprise. It also reviews a number of basic types of software programs that are used to make computers perform various tasks. The last section of this chapter deals with the problem of computer connectivity and compatibility.

Computers and Controllers

The computer can be considered the brain of the updated manufacturing enterprise and can be called the kingpin of the new technologies discussed in the preceding chapter. It constitutes the single most important ingredient that has made it possible to transform the promise of automation into practical reality.

The development of computer technology based on solid state electronics was a prerequisite for the development of today's automated factory. Computers permit manufacturing to take place in real time, i.e., the operations can be controlled based on information that is continuously collected by computers and sensors and made available instantaneously as feedback to the manufacturing process, as well as to other functions of the enterprise.

An integrated system of a large number of computers can provide for the coordination and control of all of the components of a complete manufacturing installation, and can even assist top management in the overall direction of the enterprise.

Most decisions for directing and controlling the manufacturing process can be made automatically by a computer without any involvement by a human being. Computers can eliminate the need for much of the oral and written communication among employees and the manual control of equipment that is presently required for the proper functioning of a manufacturing facility. In the final instance, the use of computers could result in an almost paperless manufacturing enterprise.

There are basically two types of computers: general-purpose "business" computers and specialized "manufacturing industry" controllers. General-purpose computers can be classified into three categories: mainframes, minicomputers, and microcomputers.

Mainframes are the largest and most powerful class of computer. In recent years their use as a "host" computer, i.e., for coordinating and controlling a number of smaller computers, has been declining somewhat. Currently mainframes are being used more for data base management and communications. They are generally characterized as noninteractive, i.e., two-way communication with the user is limited.

Minicomputers are interactive, multiuser and multitasking machines. This means that they allow for active communication with the user, can be used by several persons at once, and can be used for several tasks simultaneously. They have taken over some of the work of mainframes by acting as host computers.

Microcomputers are single-user, single-tasking machines that usually contain only a single integrated circuit. This category includes personal computers and workstations. The latter are generally more powerful than personal computers and are especially suited for use by engineers in writing, calculating, drawing, and communicating.

In recent years the distinctions between these three basic categories of general-purpose business computers have blurred considerably. Mini- and microcomputers have been upgraded and given added capabilities.

Some super minicomputers are now as powerful as some small mainframes. At the same time, some microcomputers have been equipped with a multitasking operating system and can compete with minicomputers as multitasking machines while costing less.

Other microcomputers are designed with a new type of computing process, called Reduced-Instruction-Set Computing (RISC), giving them the same power as some minicomputers. RISC simplifies the instructions that are programmed into a computer and thereby speeds up the computing process.

Upgraded microcomputers can substitute for some minicomputers. This has resulted in an added new function for minicomputers: They now are sometimes used as "servers," i.e., they back up and perform tasks for a network of smaller computers that can then share expensive printers and extensive data files as a means of reducing costs.

Another trend that is changing the traditional role of each type of computer is the shift toward decentralization. The typical hierarchical system of layers of more powerful computers controlling two or more less powerful computers in the form of a pyramidal structure is making way for a network of personal computers and workstations.

By giving these machines improved processing power and data storage and collection capabilities, such a network does not require central control by a more powerful computer. One advantage of this arrangement is that it speeds up operations by distributing processing tasks over a large number of separate computers.

In addition to the general-purpose business computers reviewed thus far, there are several types of specialized controllers utilized in manufacturing, including:

Computer Numerical Controllers (CNCs). These are dedicated computers that are integrated with a machine tool and control its operation.

Programmable Logic Controllers (PLCs). These are computers especially designed for controlling a variety of automated equipment in a discrete manufacturing process.

Process Controllers. These are computers especially designed for controlling a continuous flow manufacturing process.

CNCs consist of a central processing unit, an electromechanical servo control system, memory, input/output modules, and a display readout. They translate numerical data into positional data and motion control, generate tool path data, act as an interface between machine tools and users, and provide a communications link with supervisory computers. Sequencing tasks—such as tool changing, probe control, and torque-controlled machining—are handled by PLCs. CNCs are being upgraded and are becoming more like microcomputers, with improved user interfaces, more memory, etc.

PLCs originally were designed as a stand-alone replacement for the relays and switches that controlled assembly lines in the automotive industry. They employed relatively simple "ladder logic" instead of a more sophisticated computer language and were not quite at the same level as a business computer. However, in recent years, PLCs have been upgraded significantly, and many currently produced PLCs have the capabilities of a small computer, although they still have a special function, namely, they are dedicated to the control of equipment used in discrete manufacturing operations.

PLCs have a programmable memory for storing instructions to perform their tasks, and they contain Input/Output (I/O) modules that allow them to interface with human beings as well as with the equipment they control. PLCs have a range of capabilities and can be classified according to the number of I/O connection points, functional attributes, and memory capacity.

PLCs are ruggedly constructed, are ideally suited for a factory environment, and have a reputation for reliability and high uptime. Sophisticated PLCs are very user friendly, employ a high-level computer language, can perform floating-point math, and offer a wide range of communications options.

A third type of controller, the process controller, originated in the petrochemical industry as a pneumatic analog instrument. Like the PLCs, they have been upgraded into dedicated computers. Also known as Distributed Control Systems (DCSs), they are widely used in all types of continuous flow processes, including, e.g., petroleum refining and power generation.

It has been estimated that about 40 percent of all manufacturing processes are a hybrid of discrete- and continuous-flow operations. They include food, beverage, pharmaceuticals, fine chemicals, steel, and pulp and paper. This hybrid type of manufacturing process has become a market for both PLCs and DCSs.

Some PLCs are equipped with some of the features of DCSs, while some DCSs have been given some of the capabilities of PLCs. As a result, the distinction between PLCs and DCSs is blurring, and both types of controller are becoming substitutes for each other in mixed discrete- and continuous-flow processes. DCSs tend to be somewhat more sophisticated and efficient, but PLCs are cheaper and are more appropriate for smaller manufacturing installations.

One of the key developments in the employment of computers on the factory floor is the increasing use of general-purpose business computers. Minicomputers, personal computers, and workstations have joined PLCs and DCSs to form a new category called industrial computers.

Business computers that are used on the factory floor are typically designed more ruggedly than those employed in the office. Like PLCs and DCSs, they must be able to cope with a more hostile and variable environment, e.g., airborne particulates, shock and vibration, electric power spikes, and much wider temperature ranges.

By adding the capability of operating in real time—the traditional strong point of PLCs and DCSs—mini- and microcomputers used on the factory floor are able to take on new tasks that make them more valuable as industrial computers. They also tend to be more user friendly, e.g., by incorporating touch screens, voice recognition, or barcode input capability.

On the factory floor, minicomputers typically function at the upper level of the computer system and are used for manufacturing cell control, scheduling, materials handling, inspection, etc. However, more powerful microcomputers—especially workstations—are beginning to take on some of the functions of minicomputers.

True workstations still are not in common use on the factory floor. Many factory "workstations" are relatively simple operator interface devices with very limited capabilities, while others are really personal computers. However, full-fledged engineering-type workstations are expected to become more prominent on the factory floor because of their real-time capabilities, comparative ease of linking up with other computers, extensive graphics capabilities, high degree of processing power, and relatively low cost.

Although rapid headway continues to be made in upgrading computers and computer programs, there are two formidable computer-related obstacles that impede more rapid progress toward fully integrated automated manufacturing.

The first problem is inherent in the basic functioning of most computers: Computers today still process information sequentially, i.e., they work on one problem at a time. This type of processing is too slow and cumbersome to properly handle the demands placed on computers by a large-scale manufacturing installation.

It appears likely that this problem will eventually be resolved by equipping computers with parallel-processing capabilities. This technology greatly increases the speed at which a computer operates by making it possible to execute a large number of operations simultaneously, rather than sequentially as at present. Some progress has already been made in this direction, including the difficult task of writing special software, and more progress is expected.

The second problem consists of the lack of simple, direct computer connectivity and compatibility that would make it possible to effortlessly link all the computers in an installation into a smoothly functioning network. This topic is dealt with in the last section of this chapter.

Software

The proper functioning of computers depends on the input of various types of operating control information called software. There are three types of software instructions that are required for a computer to perform its work: machine software, systems software, and applications software.

Machine software is incorporated into the computer by its manufacturer and cannot be changed. Systems software, usually referred to as the operating system, controls the functioning of a computer and enables it to be used for executing applications software programs. Most computers can run on only one operating system—and this limits their capability of being connected to other computers that run on a different operating system.

Applications software refers to the numerous programs that can be run on a computer to accomplish various tasks. Each task or group of tasks requires a different program.

Much progress has been made in recent years in improving applications software. Vendors have made it easier, e.g., for employees who are not programming experts to customize their software by embedding application development "tools" in some of their general-purpose programs. In the meantime, the cost of many software programs has dropped significantly.

A recent software development that is gaining widespread interest is the Object-Oriented Programming System (OOPS). An OOPS software program consists of independent "intelligent" modules, i.e., reusable "building blocks" ("objects")—instead of numbers and mathematical procedures—that describe the various attributes of a particular item.

OOPS simplifies the creation of customized software programs, facilitates the process of making modifications in such programs, and makes them more reliable. However, the initial creation of objects requires careful, skillful planning. OOPS also is still limited by the absence of standards that would allow the exchange of objects among different computers.

In spite of the progress that has been made, software still remains the weak link in achieving fully integrated factory automation. Incompatible software programs used by various types of automated equipment and sold by different vendors tend to result in a lack of easy equipment connectivity within the plant, and a lack of smooth communications among the plant, office, and outside suppliers.

In planning the purchase of software programs—as well as computer hardware—it is important, therefore, to carefully evaluate how the various programs will have to mesh with each other and to make sure that the programs have compatible operating systems.

Described below are five categories of software programs that are typically employed in updating a manufacturing enterprise: computer-aided design, computer-aided manufacturing, computer-aided process planning, manufacturing resources planning, and artificial intelligence.

Computer-Aided Design

Computer-Aided Design (CAD) is one of the most widely utilized types of computer programs by manufacturing companies. Installing a CAD system often is one of the first steps taken in upgrading a manufacturing organization, and, in fact, is sometimes the only step. Even so, today many, if not most products are still designed manually, in the traditional manner, by drawing on paper and constructing solid wood or clay models.

CAD started out as an aid in drafting, and many applications of CAD are still limited to replacing manual drafting techniques. Newer terms, such as Computer-Aided Drafting and Design (CADD) and Computer-Aided Industrial Design (CAID), are sometimes used when referring to more sophisticated programs that also aid in actually designing a part or a product, including, e.g., product planning, manufacturing planning, testing, and engineering analysis. With CAD, the detailed shop drawings are produced automatically, i.e., derived directly from the design layout, and the intermediate step of preparing subassembly drawings—whether on paper or on the display screen—is eliminated.

CAD programs typically are run on engineering workstations with sophisticated graphics, including geometric modeling, visualization, and animation. The interactive computer graphics capability of the system makes it possible to create an image of a product being developed and then to store this image as a set of digital data. The image can be edited and manipulated as needed.

Most CAD systems, especially those run on workstations, have a single display screen on which "windows" can be opened to show textual information, such as directions and a "menu" of choices, next to the image of the product being designed. This makes such systems very user friendly.

CAD systems are function specific, i.e., they vary according to the type of engineering for which they will be used, e.g., electrical, structural, or mechanical. They are especially helpful in modifying designs that are already computerized, more so than in initially designing a totally new item.

The earliest and most basic CAD systems can produce only two-dimensional line images. Next generation systems can be used to prepare three-dimensional wireframe images, and today's even-more sophisticated systems can create solid, fully rendered, and shaded images in color.

Closely related to CAD is another program called Computer-Aided Engineering (CAE) that helps to check basic errors in design and to optimize the manufacturability of a product, a topic discussed in Chap. 4 under Concurrent Engineering. A major engineering task for which CAE is especially helpful is Finite Element Analysis (FEA), a method for determining stress, deflection, etc., by subdividing a part into a number of "blocks" or "elements" for analysis.

A CAD system with real-time three-dimensional modeling capability is a powerful tool that can significantly shorten the whole design process and improve the final product. Specific benefits include the following:

- The design process takes less time.
- The quality of the design is improved.
- The accuracy of the product data is improved.
- Legibility of the product data is better.
- Interference and tolerances can be checked automatically.
- The image can be animated to check function, etc.
- The image can be manipulated, including rotation, etc.
- Multiview drawings can be created automatically.
- Changes during design development can be quickly incorporated and checked out.
- Alternate designs can easily be developed and completed for comparison purposes.
- The design can be optimized by the system.
- The physical properties of the designed object can be calculated automatically.
- The system produces all the required engineering documentation.
- The system keeps track of all design changes.
- The system manages the storage of every engineering document.
- Coordination among the various people involved in the design process is facilitated, and information can be shared easily.

Perhaps even more important potentially than the benefits enumerated above is the use of CAD-generated data as input for computer-aided manufacturing, a topic discussed in the next section.

Computer-Aided Manufacturing

Computer-Aided Manufacturing (CAM) basically includes all of the programs, equipment, and methodologies involved in manufacturing the products designed on a CAD system. As such, CAM can be considered as the counterpart of CAD: Whereas CAD updates the design and engineering function, CAM is doing the same for the factory floor. Unfortunately, the link between the two types of programs—often shown as "CAD/CAM" as if they were inseparable Siamese twins—is still rather weak.

CAD was developed as an engineering department program, utilizing general-purpose business computers. CAM, on the other hand, is strictly factory based and depends on special-purpose controllers. The two types of technology and related software were originally not compatible and attempts to link the two via a common data base have only relatively recently become successful.

These technical problems are exacerbated by a lack of adequate communication between engineering and manufacturing, a topic dealt with in Chap. 4 under "Concurrent Engineering." Another obstacle is conservatism on the part of factory floor personnel who have a tendency to want to continue to plan and control the manufacturing process themselves, rather than rely on CAD-generated data.

Yet, to achieve truly and fully computer-integrated manufacturing with all its benefits, it is essential that CAD and CAM be intimately connected in such a manner that the data generated by CAD can be used directly as input for CAM. In other words, it should be possible for products designed on a CAD system to be manufactured by automated equipment without any further human intervention. As yet, this is being accomplished only in rare instances.

However, good progress is being made in improving the link between CAD and CAM and in overcoming the obstacles that tend to frustrate integration. It is expected that over the years ahead fully integrated CAD/CAD systems will be installed by a growing number of manufacturing companies. Also, it should be noted here that, even without a direct CAD/CAM link, much can be accomplished toward updating a manufacturing operation by installing a CAD or CAM or both as extremely beneficial programs in their own right.

Computer-Aided Process Planning

Computer-Aided Process Planning (CAPP) is an essential link between CAD and CAM. CAPP consists of preparing a detailed plan with instructions specifying how a product is to be manufactured and/or assembled, taking into account the characteristics of both the product and the available equipment and processes.

Process planning has a significant impact on production cost. The plan determines how effectively a company utilizes the resources at its disposal in manufacturing its products. Specific tasks performed by a CAPP program include:

- Routing and sequencing
- Selecting the machine
- Selecting the tool
- Specifying the jigs and fixtures
- Specifying the setups
- Generating numerical control programs for machine tools
- Planning tool paths
- Determining materials-handling requirements, etc.

The sophistication of CAPP programs varies considerably. There are two types of programs: variant planning and generative planning.

A CAPP program of the variant type requires the prior creation of a data base developed as part of the introduction of group technology, a topic discussed in Chap. 4. The program retrieves from this data base a plan that was prepared for a similar product or process. A human process planner then modifies this plan to fit the requirements for the new product to be manufactured or assembled.

With a generative CAPP program, a totally new process plan is created without utilizing any previous plans. In some generative programs, human planners still play a role in preparing the final plan. However, a fully automatic generative program prepares the entire detailed process plan, utilizing an expert system program, which is discussed later in this chapter under "Artificial Intelligence."

Such an advanced CAPP program contains a large data base with details about available processing equipment, as well as general manufacturing and engineering principles, e.g., machining logic, tooling knowledge, time estimates, system-programming tools, and standards.

Since CAPP is essentially a link between CAD and CAM and also interfaces with manufacturing resources planning—the master plan of a manufacturing operation, discussed in the next section—CAPP can be introduced only *after* CAD, CAM, and manufacturing resources planning have been implemented. Also, in view of these relationships, it is important to make sure when selecting a CAPP system that the system is able to interface easily with all three programs.

An advanced CAPP system produces numerous benefits in the form of savings in time, higher quality, and greater accuracy, resulting in a high return on investment in such a system. Specific benefits include:

- Much faster creation of process plans
- More rapid execution of process plans
- Increased productivity of machine tools and other equipment
- Reduced setup time
- Improved accuracy and consistency of process plans
- More accurate materials-requirements plans
- Better production scheduling and capacity planning
- Better overall manufacturing coordination
- Improved optimization of manufacturing resources
- Better cost estimates
- Better control over documentation and reduced reliance on paper records
- Less need for hard-to-find, highly experienced human process planners

The adoption of CAPP has thus far been rather limited. Most companies still rely on the accumulated, detailed knowledge of process planners. A major reason is that easy-to-use, sophisticated CAPP systems have only recently become available. Also, even the most advanced systems still do not measure up in all respects to human intelligence.

However, as the use of CAD, CAM, and other updating methods is spreading, CAPP is expected to gain increasing recognition as an essential next-step ingredient of a comprehensive factory modernization program.

Manufacturing Resources Planning

For a manufacturing company of even modest size and complexity to function effectively, it is of paramount importance for management to have in place a comprehensive manufacturing plan that assists in utilizing the company's resources to optimum advantage. Until the advent of today's computer, such planning was performed manually and left much to be desired.

Systematic operational planning started to evolve in the United States more than four decades ago from a system for tracking inventory. This slowly became more comprehensive and more formal and developed into Materials Requirements Planning (MRP) during the 1960s.

Subsequently, other functions were added to the original basic task of ordering parts and raw materials, such as capacity planning, master production planning and scheduling, shop-floor control, purchasing, order processing, and distribution planning. The last step was to convert the operational data into financial information that could be used for business planning.

By the mid-1980s, Manufacturing Resources Planning (MRP-II) had developed in the United States into an effective, flexible computer-based planning and scheduling tool for today's manufacturing enterprise. MRP-II integrates and coordinates all information-processing systems of the enterprise and covers all manufacturing operations from the receipt of raw materials to the shipment of the final product.

Unfortunately, MRP-II is applied to full advantage by only a limited number of companies thus far. Many companies do not yet recognize the potential benefit of MRP-II for their organization and still equate MRP-II with the old, now obsolete concept of MRP. Another obstacle frequently encountered by manufacturing companies is their lack of a sufficiently accurate and complete data base, a prerequisite for MRP-II.

In addition, some companies find it difficult to accommodate both Just-in-Time (JIT), a methodology discussed in Chap. 4, and MRP-II simultaneously, characterizing the former as simply a "pull" system and the latter as a "push" system. Actually, the two methodologies—if used correctly—are complementary. MRP-II provides needed annual as well as shorter term production planning, while JIT focuses on day-to-day order execution. Also, JIT is much more than an inventory-reducing materials pull system. JIT's pervasive philosophy and practice of avoiding waste and making continuous improvements are more likely to facilitate than hinder the planning tasks performed by MRP-II.

It is anticipated that MRP-II will continue to evolve with the help of more sophisticated software, possibly incorporating artificial intelligence. Especially promising are more detailed master production scheduling programs that can further improve the effectiveness of MRP-II.

It is interesting to note that Japan has begun to adopt MRP-II as a planning tool in coordination with JIT, in an effort to make JIT more flexible and to provide a planning framework for utilizing JIT more effectively.

To successfully introduce MRP-II, or any of the other updating methodologies and technologies reviewed in this book, in a manufacturing organization requires companywide commitment and unstinting allocation of resources. Each company will have to develop its own specific brand of MRP-II, based on its own unique needs.

Artificial Intelligence

Artificial Intelligence (AI) is only recently being recognized as a highly worthwhile tool for an automated manufacturing operation. As the term implies, AI is a type of computer program that attempts to mimic the thinking process of the human brain. It can be used to solve certain types of problems, understand images, plan programs, recognize speech, and interpret complex, incomplete, and even conflicting data.

The most successful and most developed form of AI thus far is the Expert System (ES). Today a number of ES programs are being used in manufacturing, and they have proven to be extremely cost-effective.

ES programs—also known as rule-based programs—are created by accumulating a large number of rules of thumb derived from the knowledge of experts in a particular specialty. This information is combined with a set of instructions for manipulating the data. By applying "if/then" questions, such programs can provide advice, diagnose problems, provide possible solutions, and even make decisions, e.g., to control automated equipment without human intervention. One such application of ES, namely, to CAPP, was mentioned in a previous subsection of this chapter dealing with CAM.

Neural network programs are another form of AI. Still mostly in a developmental stage, these programs—unlike conventional computer programs—process multiple instructions simultaneously, rather than sequentially, and store information in patterns of interconnections, rather than in bits of discrete information. As such, they tend to resemble the way the human brain functions.

One type of neural network program is labeled *fuzzy logic*. It is able to deal with probabilities and uncertainties, as opposed to the "yes/no" type of logic to which a conventional computer program is limited. Fuzzy logic, once it is fully developed, is expected to have wide application in the real world, including manufacturing, where information often is incomplete and tentative.

Still another form of AI that is being developed is speech recognition, a technology already mentioned in "Data Collection Technologies" in Chap. 2. Such a program attempts to recognize the patterns and logic that are common in all human speech and to interpret each person's distinct way of speaking. Speech recognition programs are likely to become helpful in manufacturing by freeing workers from having to use their hands to control automated equipment by means of keyboards.

However, for the time being, ESs are the only form of AI that has direct application to manufacturing. ES programs have been greatly upgraded over the past several years. They now run on standard hardware platforms and are able to absorb data from a wide variety of information sources.

ESs also have acquired the speed and agility to direct and control online specific production processes based on information that the ES has received and analyzed in real time. Such control can be applied to automated assembly, machining, robots, and materials handling. Other applications of ES include such functions as production scheduling, inspection, quality control, preventive maintenance, and even product planning and customer service. Basically, ES increases the degree of flexibility of automated equipment and helps it to acquire a bit more of the outstanding advantage of the human worker, i.e., his or her intelligence.

Computer Connectivity and Compatibility

The concept of "open systems"—as contrasted with proprietary systems—is of key importance in selecting computers and software for an updating project. Open systems are based on stable, publicly defined standards for hardware and software.

The ultimate goal of open systems is total, simple connectivity and compatibility of all computers and software, i.e., a situation where all computers can be linked together without any special bridging devices and all software programs can be run on any computer—regardless of its manufacturer. Unfortunately, this goal is far from being reached.

The concept of open systems has several applications, including intracompany communications, intercompany communications, and computer operating systems. These three applications are discussed here.

Local Communications Networks

Until relatively recently, computers were used singly, i.e., they were not linked up to each other in any kind of network configuration. Since prior to about 1980 there was no need for computers to communicate with each other, no attempts were made to provide connectivity among computers made by different manufacturers. In fact, manufacturers often purposely made their computers incompatible for competitive reasons. However, with the development of the various technologies, methodologies, and computer programs that are being utilized to update the manufacturing enterprise—combined with the resulting heavy emphasis on systems integration—computer connectivity has become crucial.

A fully integrated automated manufacturing organization requires an effective, comprehensive, integrated network of computer and equipment links that allows every function in the enterprise to be performed under integrated computer control. This includes such functions as order processing, shipping, scheduling, inventory control, and materials handling, as well as the operation of shop-floor equipment. This network ideally should feature "seamless" connectivity, i.e., it should have as few special linking devices as possible, and must be capable of operating in real time.

Such a network typically consists of a number of subnetworks for specific areas of the organization, such as the factory floor, the engineering department, and the various office functions. Simple but effective linkage among these three areas continues to be difficult to achieve, partly as a result of the different orientations of the people in these three areas, and partly due to the different types of computer equipment being used.

A network or subnetwork of computers within a company—whether in one location or in several locations within a few miles of each other—is called a Local Area Network (LAN). If the network includes more distant locations, it is referred to as a Wide Area Network (WAN).

A network of computers can be more than just a means of exchanging information. By linking up, for example, several general-purpose personal computers and workstations together with one or more specialized so-called server computers and peripheral equipment, the network becomes a powerful, integrated tool, known as a "client-server network."

Such an arrangement allows individual small computers to collaborate as a team by sharing software programs and hardware (e.g., a laser printer), distributing data, monitoring each other's output, and delegating certain tasks, e.g., heavy computing or managing a data base for use by the other computers in the network, to a server computer.

Client-server networks sometimes include hundreds of microcomputers and can perform as well as, and often better than, big mainframes and minicomputers. In fact, such networks are gradually replacing mainframes and minicomputers in many applications. They are more responsive and flexible, they can easily be expanded by adding more computers, and they cost less. Their capability derives to a large extent from their use of the same powerful microprocessor chips that are utilized in mainframes.

In order to be able to simply link a variety of computers and subnetworks into a single, interactive communications network, all these components must share a common set of communications standards. If they do not do so, a host of special linking devices must be employed that tend to make the communications system more complex, more costly, and less efficient. Such devices include protocol converters, routers, bridges, etc.

Unfortunately, equipment manufacturers have developed a variety of proprietary communications systems that are not compatible and that prevent their equipment from being connected directly to that of other manufacturers. As a result, many manufacturing companies today are burdened with incompatible, multiprotocol networks that are interconnected by means of a large number of bridging devices.

In an effort to resolve this problem, the International Standards Organization has developed an Open Systems Interconnection (OSI) model that provides a basic framework for devising sets of more specific communication rules, known as protocols, that are "open," i.e., not proprietary. Such protocols provide for the direct and orderly transmission of information within and among LANs. The framework consists of seven layers, each addressing a different aspect of connectivity, including, e.g., standards for the physical linkage and for addressing techniques.

In 1980, General Motors took the initiative to start developing such an OSI protocol for use on the factory floor. The protocol that finally resulted from a 5-year effort of a GM-sponsored computer user group is a token-passing bus protocol,[1] known as the Manufacturing Automation Protocol (MAP). It defines basic communications system standards for computers and software programs used on the factory floor.

A MAP network typically runs on a broadband copper cable. However, some companies have begun to use a fiber optic cable instead of broadband, and it appears that fiber optics will gradually replace broadband. Fiber has several advantages over copper: it is not affected by electromagnetic and radio-frequency interference, it is more reliable, and such a system does not require repeaters within the factory building.

Following the example set by General Motors, the Boeing Company developed another open protocol based on the OSI model for use by networks in the office, known as the Technical Office Protocol (TOP). TOP is compatible with MAP and, in fact, acts as the counterpart of MAP in that it provides communications standards for the rest of the

---

[1]A token-passing bus is a method for avoiding the simultaneous sending of information by several terminals connected to a bus network. A "token" is circulated among the terminals on a regular basis; only the terminal that has the token can send information.

manufacturing enterprise. TOP also helps to establish a crucial direct link between the two network systems.

With MAP and TOP, a network bus replaces a large number of point-to-point cables, and a single software program replaces different programs for each dissimilar piece of equipment. The implementation of both MAP and TOP allows the creation of a truly integrated communications system, featuring a direct interchange of information with a minimum of costly and inefficient special bridging devices.

Since MAP and TOP greatly facilitate communications among a variety of automated equipment, they could well become practically prerequisites when updating a manufacturing operation. However, for the time being, MAP is not yet being implemented widely. Reasons for this lag include the following:

- MAP is much more expensive and more difficult to install than proprietary alternatives.

- MAP requires voluminous documentation (some 350 pages of specifications for MAP's latest 3.0 version).

- MAP may not have reached its final version. The 3.0 version has been purposely frozen until 1994 to eliminate apprehension that it will quickly become obsolete.

- MAP is more comprehensive and complex than what is needed by many manufacturers at this time.

Several proprietary network systems are well entrenched, including Ethernet and DECnet. Such systems are not likely to be replaced in the foreseeable future by MAP, especially not in applications where these cheaper systems are adequate for the tasks to be performed.

In the long run, however, it is generally expected that OSI-based protocols, most likely MAP and TOP, will gain wide acceptance. Because MAP and TOP offer the only open protocols available for direct connectivity and efficient communications among otherwise incompatible equipment, these two protocols should be seriously considered when establishing totally new communications systems, especially when they are to be a component of a comprehensive updating and automation program.

Electronic Data Interchange

In addition to the intracompany communications networks discussed in the preceding section, a need for directly linking the internal networks of a manufacturing company to those of its suppliers and customers has developed. As a result, a technology known as Electronic Data Interchange (EDI) is being employed. Although originally introduced some 20 years ago, EDI started to generate widespread interest only around 1986. Its main applications are in the automotive industry and in retailing where it is used in connection with that industry's quick response program, a topic covered in "Quick Response" in Chap. 4.

EDI is the computer-to-computer electronic exchange of business data between trading partners. At present, many companies use a variety of proprietary communications standards in linking their internal networks to each other for this purpose, and this limits the spread of EDI.

However, several years ago, a start was made to try to introduce a single, uniform EDI communications standard, namely, X 12, which would hopefully gradually replace the various proprietary EDI standards. Progress in adopting X 12 has been slow, but it is anticipated that this standard will be generally used in the coming years.

Fortunately, EDI standards are much simpler than LAN protocols. They only cover the format of the information being transmitted and do not refer to its content. As a result, the lack of uniform EDI standards presents less of an obstacle to linking networks that are based on different standards.

EDI can be used to transmit a wide range of information between two companies concerning the purchase, specification and movement of, and the payment for raw materials, parts, components, and finished products. Functional departments that can be involved in this exchange of information include purchasing, inventory control, production scheduling, engineering, logistics, shipping, accounting, etc.

If it is implemented to optimum advantage, EDI can greatly benefit a manufacturing enterprise. EDI is especially appropriate for trading partners that transact a high volume of repetitive business with each other. Specific benefits include:

- Reduced paper flow and lower paper processing costs
- Increased data accuracy and less error tracking and correction
- Lower order processing costs
- Lower inventories and better inventory control
- Lower manpower requirements
- More efficient production scheduling
- Improved cash flow

- Faster response time from suppliers
- Faster response to changes in market demand
- Easier implementation of a just-in-time program (discussed in Chap. 4)
- Better relationships among manufacturers, suppliers, and retailers
- Improved customer service and higher customer satisfaction

EDI systems are typically installed by suppliers at the urging of large manufacturers to which they sell raw materials, parts, or components. In fact, EDI is currently a standard requirement for vendors who want to do business with the big three automobile manufacturers.

However, many small manufacturers still tend to shy away from EDI. Establishing an effective EDI network is a complex and time-consuming effort that significantly affects the way in which a company operates.

A fully implemented EDI system requires very close cooperation between trading partners and unrestricted access to each other's data bases, as well as disclosure of their production and marketing plans. It also involves electronically linking the vendor's production scheduling to its customer's estimated order scheduling, automatically recording a transaction in accounts payable and receivable, issuing checks for payment, etc.

Such a total implementation of EDI has been very limited thus far, even among small manufacturers that have established obligatory EDI links with their large customers. In practice, many such small vendors treat the EDI system at their end as if it were a simple fax system. They either rekey the incoming EDI information for further automatic processing or, even more frequently, process this information as they would non-EDI information. By doing so, they do not gain any of the benefits of an EDI system, even though they are linked into it.

Ideally, EDI is integrated with an automated identification system such as bar coding. Although EDI by itself does not require bar coding, the latter greatly improves EDI's effectiveness. However, adding an automatic identification system to EDI could pose a difficult problem for vendors that sell to several large customers, each of which may have its own, different bar-code standard.

Most EDI systems that have been installed thus far utilize only a small fraction of the technology's total capability. However, in its most advanced form, EDI has the potential of becoming a significant component of a comprehensively updated and automated manufacturing sector.

EDI already acts as a vital link for groups of mutually interdependent manufacturers and retailers, and its use is spreading rapidly. Every manufacturing company that is planning an updating program should at least consider the possibility of establishing EDI links with some of its major suppliers and customers.

Computer Operating Systems

As mentioned in the introduction to the Software section in this chapter, the basic functioning of a computer is controlled by systems software, usually called the operating system. Computer manufacturers have developed a number of proprietary operating systems, most of which are incompatible with each other. This means that applications software programs written for one operating system can usually be run only on a computer that features that particular operating system.

Incompatible proprietary operating systems make it difficult, if not impossible, and expensive for customers to mix and match computers from different vendors, thereby reducing the customers' choice of equipment and software. This limits competition and keeps prices high.

Demands by computer users for open operating systems have resulted in several initiatives by computer manufacturers to standardize their equipment. One such initiative has produced an open, standardized operating system called UNIX. Another group of computer manufacturers—suspecting that the UNIX standards might favor members of the UNIX development group and fearing a loss of market share—developed another open system, called OSF/1, to compete with UNIX.

To add to the confusion, a number of other computer manufacturers have developed some 28 variants of UNIX, each of which usually requires the software program to be at least slightly modified in order to make it compatible with the other UNIX variants.

The basic problem is that most computer manufacturers have been less than enthusiastic about promoting truly open systems since widespread adoption of such systems would reduce their competitive advantage. Another problem is that a significant investment has already been made by many manufacturing companies in computers and software that are based on proprietary systems.

The upshot is that, for the time being, open and proprietary systems will have to coexist. Most of the personal computers that are installed in manufacturing companies utilize a single proprietary system, called DOS, which has become a de facto standard for personal computers used in manufacturing. For many applications where personal computers are employed, there is no need for a more powerful and more sophisticated operating system such as UNIX.

In contrast, UNIX is the preferred operating system for workstations, which are rapidly increasing in number. This means that special linkages are required between these two types of computers as well as with other types of computers employed for other functions in the enterprise that are also not based on UNIX.

UNIX is the most open operating system available and has several advantages over most other systems, including the following:

- Multitasking capability
- Relatively easy networking capability
- Relatively easy to translate, i.e., "port," software written for one system for use on another system
- Availability of UNIX-based applications software programs
- Adaptability to real-time operations on the factory floor

In recent years, a definite trend has been developing among manufacturing companies toward open systems and away from proprietary systems. Many manufacturers have begun to insist on UNIX as the operating system for their company. Also, the number of UNIX-based software programs that are being put on the market has been increasing. It is likely, therefore, that UNIX will become the dominant operating system in manufacturing over the years ahead, not only on the factory floor but also in the office.

Ultimately, each manufacturing company embarking upon an updating program must evaluate with the help of computer experts which system or systems will be most appropriate for its unique requirements and circumstances.

4
Manufacturing Methodologies

A number of new approaches to manufacturing are at least as important as new equipment and software. In fact, it is practically impossible to make effective use of new equipment without applying at least some of these new methodologies. Interestingly enough, the reverse is *not* true: The new approaches can be, and have been, applied to great advantage in updating a manufacturing enterprise without installing any automated equipment.

This is at least partly a result of highly effective competition from abroad and has been aided by the rapid development of several of the sophisticated technologies reviewed in the preceding two chapters. U.S. manufacturers have begun to shift the emphasis of their competitive efforts from cost control to customer satisfaction.

This new emphasis covers intermediate customers as well as final (retail) customers, and has taken four distinct forms:

1. *More Product Customization.* Customers today demand greater choice in product features and faster response to changing tastes and preferences; this requires greater manufacturing flexibility and faster new product development.

2. *Better Product Quality.* Each separate member of the production and distribution chain as well as the final consumer demand better product quality and fewer "lemons."

3. *Faster Order Processing.* The same members also expect their suppliers to ship ordered materials, supplies, and merchandise much more quickly than in the past.

4. *Better Customer Service.* Customers expect better follow-up after the sale and better warranties.

This new emphasis on customer satisfaction requires a complete change in attitude on the part of everyone in the organization—a difficult and time-consuming process. The new orientation of effort can be characterized as time- and quality-based competition. It indirectly also affects cost-based competition, since many of the methodologies used to cater to better customer satisfaction also tend to lower costs.

Another interesting and beneficial effect of this change in emphasis for U.S. manufacturers is an increase in their competitiveness relative to manufacturers abroad. The latter will be at a growing disadvantage for at least three reasons:

1. Their greater distance from their customers will make it almost impossible for manufacturers abroad to respond and react as quickly to changes in market demand as manufacturers in the United States.

2. The spreading adoption of automated flexible manufacturing in the United States will cause a continuing drop in direct labor cost as a percentage of total cost, and this will erode the advantage of countries with low labor rates.

3. The introduction of ever more sophisticated manufacturing technologies in the United States will be hard to match by low-wage undercapitalized countries.

Three time-oriented methodologies, just-in-time, concurrent engineering, and quick response, as well as two other new approaches that are important components of a comprehensive updating program, group technology and total quality control, are reviewed in this chapter. Two other concepts that are basic to automation, flexible and cellular manufacturing, are discussed in Chap. 5.

Group Technology

The concept of Group Technology (GT) was developed originally by Frederick Taylor and others in the 1920s, but did not come into general use until rather recently. GT is a method for improving the productivity of a manufacturing operation by grouping the products to be manufactured into "families" according to common characteristics. It is an essential part of a successful updating program that should be dealt with early in the planning process.

Although GT is suitable for many types of manufacturing operations, it can be especially cost-effective for manufacturers of discrete metal products employing a batch process, introducing many new product varieties each year or many new product types or models, making products to order, or purchasing many proprietary items. It is not suitable for high volumes of single products where equipment utilization justifies a dedicated production line.

The simplest but least accurate grouping method consists of having experienced personnel analyze each product. A slightly more accurate method involves a review of each product's routing sheet. However, the most commonly used method requires a formal parts classification and coding process known as Production Flow Analysis (PFA). This process is difficult and time-consuming but is the most appropriate method in the majority of cases. PFA groups all parts, products, workpieces, and assemblies according to certain characteristics and assigns a code to each family of items and each item within this family.

Depending on the primary use of GT in each manufacturing facility, the grouping is done according to design similarities or manufacturing similarities. Design attributes include dimensions, tolerances, geometry, material, etc. Manufacturing attributes cover weight and size, production processes, operational sequence, applicable tools and fixtures, processing duration, batch size, etc.

A grouping according to design attributes is used in cases where the emphasis is on minimizing the creation of new part designs. If GT is planned to result in a rearrangement of the manufacturing process, a grouping according to manufacturing attributes is usually preferable. Sometimes a combination of the two types of groupings is used.

GT started out as a manual process, and this process is still useful in small-scale applications without being computerized. When the number of new parts to be classified exceeds 5000 per year, computerization of the classifications and codes that have been developed is helpful. When the number reaches 10,000, computerization becomes essential. Unfortunately, no software program exists that can create a GT classification system without considerable human effort.

GT is based on a relatively simple concept. However, the process of developing and implementing a GT classification and coding program is extremely complex and difficult. As a result, the task is very costly and time-consuming—often taking several years. Also, once introduced, the system must continue to be improved and expanded to cover new products. Several software programs are available that can help set up the program, but since the system must be custom designed, most of the work must still be performed by the manufacturer's in-house staff.

Nevertheless, GT is making headway among U.S. manufacturing com-panies because its advantages are indisputable and significant. Basically, GT simplifies the manufacturing process and lowers costs by reducing variety and duplication, increasing equipment utilization, and improv-ing orderliness and visibility.

A GT program is often undertaken as an essential first step in reor-ganizing a conventional manufacturing installation—in which ma-chines with the same function are grouped together—into what is known as a "cellular manufacturing arrangement" in which each work cell is devoted to process or assemble a family of products. Cellular manufacturing is discussed in more detail in Chap. 5.

Although GT is a prerequisite for introducing cellular manufactur-ing, it provides a number of valuable benefits in its own right, whether or not the layout of a manufacturing installation is subsequently radi-cally altered to accommodate cellular manufacturing.

With the continuing shift from mass-production manufacturing to small- and medium-size batch-type manufacturing in response to chang-ing market demand, the upfront fixed cost of preparing for the manu-facture of a new product is becoming an increasingly heavier burden. By utilizing GT, this fixed cost can be reduced significantly. When the shift to GT is followed by a change to cellular manufacturing and the introduction of other components of an updating program, the fixed cost can be cut even further. A very low fixed cost, in turn, makes it pos-sible to reduce the size of a batch to as small as a single item.

The specific benefits of GT are diverse and include the following:

- GT improves the tracking of the large number of parts in a typical manufacturing installation.
- GT increases equipment utilization.
- GT allows the quick identification of suitable alternate parts, helps purchasing, reduces inventory, and simplifies design retrieval.
- Since most new products typically consist of 40 percent old parts, 40 percent modified old parts, and only 20 percent totally new parts, GT can greatly reduce design and manufacturing cost by drastically re-ducing the amount of time spent on designing new products. This is done by utilizing previously designed parts and assemblies.
- Setup and processing time are reduced by grouping similar parts. Grouping also makes it possible to share setups and machine tools. Design standardization, easier and better value engineering, better cost-estimating data, and less and faster materials handling are some other benefits.

- Advanced applications of GT with its extensive data base covering all aspects of the manufacturing function can be extended to manufacturing-process planning, capacity-utilization planning, and support of marketing and sales.

GT is an important basic tool in updating today's manufacturing enterprise as well as a prerequisite for introducing cost-effective automation. However, besides being costly and time-consuming, a full-fledged GT program has a pervasive impact on an enterprise, and its adoption, therefore, needs to be carefully considered by top management before being embarked upon.

Just-in-Time

Just-in-Time (JIT) is another key ingredient in the process of updating a manufacturing enterprise. JIT shares several characteristics with GT and, in fact, the two approaches work hand in glove. They both:

- Reduce costs through simplification
- Improve efficiency by eliminating waste and unnecessary actions
- Reduce inventory and storage
- Are basically very simple, common-sense approaches to manufacturing
- Do not require computerization per se; computerization becomes essential only in large installations
- Affect every function of the enterprise
- Are practically mandatory for a successful updating and automation program
- Can help improve the effectiveness and profitability of a manufacturing enterprise, even *without* automating the manufacturing installation

JIT originated as a type of manual inventory-control system with a single basic premise: Arrange to have materials and parts available for use in the manufacturing process only in the exact quantities needed at a specific time. This is a revolutionary departure from the conventional approach of storing excess supplies of all materials and parts as insurance against running out and having to halt the production process.

JIT means changing from a "push" system of producing as much as possible at high capacity levels to a "pull" system. In the pull system, goods are produced only to the extent dictated by demand and materials and parts are acquired only to the extent needed for operating at those production levels.

The Japanese have made extensive use of JIT, especially in their automotive sector where it is known as "kanban," i.e., a "sign" that is posted when the inventory of a particular item begins to run low. In the United States, JIT is also known as Continuous Flow Manufacturing (CFM).

As presently employed, JIT extends far beyond inventory control and affects all functions of a manufacturing enterprise. JIT has become a new corporate culture, an operating philosophy that can be extremely effective in upgrading a manufacturing organization and making it more efficient and profitable.

JIT in the widest sense represents a revolutionary concept in manufacturing that includes a strong commitment to excellence and continuous improvement in productivity and customer service. Every type of waste is minimized, and every action that does not add value to the final product is eliminated. Specific subgoals and benefits include:

- Less inventory
- Less work in process
- Fewer defects
- Less rework
- Fewer rejects
- Less scrap
- Fewer setups
- Less setup time
- Less handling
- Less transporting
- Less excess output
- Less surging (through better synchronization)
- Shorter lead times
- Fewer breakdowns (through better maintenance)

It should be noted that inventories can never be completely eliminated. The volume to be kept on hand will depend on the type and size of the manufacturing operation and on the specific items involved, e.g., the inventory of high-volume, expensive items can be kept very low while that of low-volume, inexpensive items should be much higher.

The introduction of JIT into a manufacturing operation is a far-reaching process that profoundly affects the whole organization. JIT should be implemented in small steps on a continuing basis, activity by activity. The process is intrusive and time-consuming, and requires a company-wide sustained, intensive effort that is spearheaded by a resourceful project leader.

Like all updating programs, JIT requires a carefully orchestrated training and education effort. Everyone involved, i.e., practically every employee, must be made aware of what is being done, its purpose, the changes that will be made, how these changes will affect the employee, and what is expected of the employee.

JIT can be—but does not have to be—just one component of a comprehensive updating program. However, to be effective, JIT must be preceded by a significant upgrading of quality control throughout the organization, to be accomplished by implementing a total quality control program, discussed in the next section.

In addition, the introduction of JIT should be accompanied by several other action programs as follows:

- Reducing lead time in production scheduling, e.g., by changing to smaller lot sizes and continuous flow of materials and work in process
- Overhauling the layout of the manufacturing process, typically by applying GT
- Upgrading preventive maintenance
- Realigning supplier relationships, i.e., fewer suppliers, longer-term contracts, quicker response, and consistently high quality of deliveries

Prior to starting a JIT program, it is necessary to make a comprehensive evaluation of the company's present capabilities that are relevant to JIT. Such an evaluation should cover the company's operations, its organization, and the market for its products. Operational information should include, e.g., equipment data, inventory levels, flow-process data, rejection rates, and order-processing time. Organizational strengths to be reviewed include engineering skills and adequacy of interdepartmental communications and cooperation.

Interestingly enough, the process of doing all of this usually exposes a large number of weaknesses and problems in the manufacturing installation that were previously hidden from view. The benefits of going through this process—and remedying the problems that are uncovered—often are significant by themselves, even before the benefits of JIT are felt.

Total Quality Control

Total Quality Control (TQC) is a management technique that has become increasingly important in recent years as a vital ingredient in any successful updating program and as a prerequisite for JIT. The two techniques are complementary: whereas a JIT program uncovers problems related to quality as it proceeds step by step, TQC solves each of these problems.

TQC is another aspect of the new manufacturing philosophy of commitment to excellence. It includes the concepts of continuous improvement, higher reliability, and better consistency in delivered product and service. It also introduces a significant new approach by transferring responsibility for quality from quality control specialists to everyone in the organization.

Quality essentially means conformance to requirements. Requirements ultimately are determined by the final consumer through the process of competition.

There are two types of product quality: quality of design, i.e., planning for quality, and quality of production, i.e., execution according to plan. There has been a tendency to overlook the first type, yet TQC should start with simplifying product design and making the product robust enough to withstand variations in the production process.

TQC was pioneered several decades ago by W. Edwards Deming. His ideas were originally rejected in the United States but found avid acceptance in Japan, starting in the 1950s. Two other prominent TQC proponents and consultants are Joseph M. Juran and Genichi Taguchi.

In the typical American factory, locating and correcting errors is a major cost item occupying up to one-quarter of its workforce. To this must be added the expense of repairing or replacing defective products that were sold. It has been estimated that inadequate quality control may result in a loss of 25 percent of a company's sales.

Many top executives of U.S. manufacturing companies grossly underestimate the importance of high quality on their competitiveness. Surveys indicate that a large number of top executives have no idea of the cost of poor quality or believe that it costs their company less than 5 percent of sales.

A majority of these executives feel that they do not need to improve the quality of their products. It is not surprising, therefore, that only about one-fourth of the total number of U.S. manufacturing companies are estimated to have introduced an effective TQC program. Many companies still use sample inspection, manual charting, and other outdated quality control techniques. The considerable lag of the United States in quality control behind several other countries, especially Japan, is a major reason for the decline in our competitiveness.

TQC constitutes a change from "defect management," i.e., locating and repairing or discarding defective products, to "reducing defects," thereby reducing the cost of quality inspection, rework, and scrappage. This basically simple change can result in enormous gains in manufacturing effectiveness.

Reducing the number of defects requires a shift of emphasis from inspecting final products to continuously monitoring the processing of parts and the assembly of the final product, and ensuring higher quality parts and higher quality manufacturing equipment. This means that TQC will involve not only the manufacturing operation but also the vendors that supply the materials, parts, and equipment. Each manufacturer must forge new vendor relationships that are based on new agreements. These agreements should guarantee that the quality of the supplied items will conform to the standards established by the manufacturing company.

Since more quality problems originate in the office than in the plant and since quality is a companywide concern, TQC should be applied to *all* functions and departments of the organization—including engineering, marketing and sales, as well as manufacturing.

The first step in preparing for a TQC program is to determine what the customer wants. The next step is to plan how to satisfy these requirements. The final step is to formulate and implement the actual TQC program to ensure that the final output conforms to the requirements.

TQC usually involves establishing a Statistical Process Control (SPC) system. SPC employs a set of sophisticated statistical analyses to detect potential problems before they occur with the aim of removing the causes of variation in the quality of the output. To use SPC effectively requires extensive training of shop floor personnel. If implemented in a practical manner and used as a problem-solving tool, SPC can be very effective in raising a company's overall quality.

A TQC program also may include the formation of one or more groups of employees that concentrate on tackling specific quality issues and/or try to resolve certain operational problems. Each company will have to develop its own TQC program that best fits its needs and preferences.

The long-term beneficial effects of a successful TQC program are widespread and will permeate the whole organization. The cost of manufacturing quality products will drop significantly due to, e.g., less inspection, less waste, fewer rejects, less rework, and lower warranty expense; employee morale will improve; the organization and its members will become more unified and cooperation oriented in pursuing corporate philosophy and objectives; and consumers will notice the improved quality of the final product, and this will result eventually in increased sales.

Like most other components of a comprehensive updating program, TQC requires a strong commitment and involvement by top management and is time-consuming. It requires a companywide new attitude toward quality and a significant change in the conventional approach to manufacturing.

Installing an effective TQC program can take several years and involves considerable training and education of employees at all levels, starting with the Chief Executive Officer (CEO). Once installed, the implementation of the program must be continuously monitored and its results measured and reported.

Concurrent Engineering

The product development process of U.S. manufacturing companies typically consists of a number of distinct, sequential steps, each performed by a different department. The marketing department originates the concept for a new product. The design engineering department designs the product. Manufacturing engineers then determine how to manufacture the parts, and process engineers develop the assembly process. Procurement arranges to obtain the various components that will be purchased. Facility engineers select the materials-handling equipment and prepare the plant layout. Marketing and sales promote and sell the product.

This departmentalization of functions was adopted especially by large organizations in an attempt to reap the benefits of specialization and thereby improve efficiency. Unfortunately, it resulted instead in raising development costs and lengthening the time it takes for a new product to reach the market place.

Although original design typically accounts for only about 5 percent of a product's cost, the design predetermines up to 90 percent of the total cost. However, in the traditional sequential process, the design department tends to concentrate on form and function, and to disregard manufacturability and other considerations. As a result, a lengthy and costly iterative follow-up process is required that involves making numerous design changes to satisfy each of the departments that play a role in developing a new product.

Over the past 15 years, a powerful "new" tool has been developed that is becoming a vital component of an effective manufacturing updating program. Concurrent Engineering (CE), also known as "simultaneous engineering," represents a move away from functional departmentalization by substituting team effort among all those involved in the product-development process.

CE attempts to integrate design, manufacturing, production, procurement, quality control, and marketing from the very beginning of the product-development process into a close-knit team effort. This team should also include outside suppliers of materials, parts, and components, as well as the manufacturers of the necessary production equipment. In addition, close links must be maintained with management, human resources, and accounting.

The effectiveness of CE can be improved by installing special information systems and employing CE software packages that facilitate communications among the various functional groups that are involved in developing new products.

CE clearly is people-oriented and requires a drastic change in a company's organization and mode of operation, as well as a significant improvement in communications within and among functional departments. The new emphasis on teamwork is likely to result in problems in the human resources area that will have to be resolved. Compensation policies, incentives, and recruitment criteria may have to be adjusted to promote team effort, and training may be needed to change attitudes and behavior.

The potential benefits of an effective CE program have been proven to be spectacular. They include better products, lower cost, higher product quality, and a shorter market lead time.

CE focuses on a number of specific objectives, such as:

- Design to meet market requirements
- Design for manufacturability
- Design for assembly
- Design for automation
- Design for product reliability
- Design for product maintainability and serviceability
- Use fewer, more standardized and interchangeable parts in the manufacturing process
- Use robust manufacturing processes and product designs
- Design for modularity

- Balance among alternative designs based on cost versus quality and other criteria
- Continuously improve the product and the production process

The second and third objectives require some clarification. Design for Manufacturability (DFM) and Design for Assembly (DFA) refer to two of the principal advantages to be derived from CE, i.e., making it easier to manufacture and assemble the product. For optimum benefit, the two objectives should be pursued in combination—Design for Manufacturability and Assembly (DFMA)—from the time the new product is first conceptualized.

Although assembly often accounts for a major portion of total product cost, DFA has had little application thus far among U.S. manufacturers.

The following are a few specific guidelines for implementing DFA:

- Reduce the number of fastening steps
- Provide for subassemblies
- Avoid difficult and complex assembly maneuvers
- Provide for a simple assembly sequence, e.g., layer by layer
- Limit the need for lifting and rotating
- Provide easy access for each part to be inserted
- Utilize gravity by assembling top-down
- Eliminate fasteners, e.g., by using snap-fit parts where possible
- Standardize fasteners
- Design parts that are easy to handle, e.g., that are not flexible and do not tangle
- Design parts that are symmetrical for easier orientation
- Avoid close tolerances
- Design parts that mate or nest easily
- Provide orientation points, guide pins, and guide surfaces to facilitate insertion
- Design parts that are not adversely affected by slight variations in characteristics, such as weld strength
- Keep the bulk and weight of the product to a minimum

It should be noted that the application of DFA does not necessarily result in a simplification of the parts to be assembled—in fact, often the opposite is true. To facilitate assembly, features may have to be added to a part that will make it easier to handle, orient, insert, and/or mate it with other parts. Also, a complex part may be specified that will substitute for two or more simpler parts, and thus one or more assembly steps can be eliminated.

Although the term concurrent engineering made its appearance as a new buzzword only relatively recently, the practice it represents is actually quite old. CE as a concept is truly American in origin as well as in application. It is said to have been used by Henry Ford in developing his famous and successful Model T vehicle early this century. Another automotive pioneer who recognized and applied the concept is Walter P. Chrysler.

During World War II, the U.S. manufacturing sector was called upon to develop military hardware within extremely short time frames. This often was accomplished successfully, and concurrent engineering played a vital role.

Unfortunately, the effective application of CE declined significantly starting around 1955 and was replaced by functional departmentalization. It was not until about 15 years ago that the concepts of CE and DFMA were gradually rediscovered by major U.S. manufacturers. Ford Motor Company became an enthusiastic supporter in 1984 and has begun to rely heavily on this approach in developing new car models.

A number of special software packages have been developed that facilitate the introduction of CE and DFMA programs. Computer-aided design, computer-aided engineering, and artificial intelligence can play important roles in this process.

The initial cost of CE and DFMA can be considerable. Besides the expense of acquiring any needed additional hardware and software, a substantial investment will have to be made in training, education, coordination, and organizational restructuring. However, as indicated previously, the potential benefits far outweigh the costs, and CE must be considered an essential component of an effective, well-rounded updating program. Each company must develop its own unique brand of CE that is best suited to its circumstances, preferences, and corporate culture.

Quick Response

Quick Response (QR) constitutes another aspect of time-based competition. The concept was introduced in the mid-1980s by Millikin and Company—a large integrated textile manufacturer—as a method for making it possible to respond much more quickly to changes in consumer buying preferences and thereby also to reduce inventories.

QR originally was limited to the textile and apparel industries. However, now it has expanded to cover almost any product sold through department stores and large retail chains such as Sears, Roebuck and Co. and K Mart Discount Stores.

By electronically transmitting retail sales information collected at checkout counters to the manufacturer and/or distributors of each item of merchandise, the manufacturers and distributors are able to immediately adjust their production and distribution schedules to reflect current market demand, cut inventories, and reduce the volume of slow-selling merchandise that must be disposed of at sizable markdowns.

By establishing similar linkages between manufacturers and their suppliers of raw materials and components, other units in the vertical production and distribution system are able to reap the same benefits. The pipelines of the distribution system become more responsive and, in effect, are shortened for each individual product. It is often possible to eliminate one or more of the intermediate distribution steps, such as accumulating merchandise in manufacturers', distributors', or retailers' distribution centers.

QR requires two modern technologies: bar coding and Electronic Data Interchange (EDI). Bar coding was discussed in Chap. 2 under "Data Collection Technologies," and EDI was discussed in Chap. 3 under "Computer Connectivity and Compatibility."

Each product and each shipping container is coded for easy tracking, using standard bar-code formats. The coded label is scanned at each checkpoint on the journey of the product or its container, i.e., at the manufacturer's shipping dock, at receiving and shipping docks of warehouses and/or distribution centers, at the receiving dock of the retailer, and at the cash register where the item is sold.

The EDI network transmits marketing and sales information in a two-way interchange between the involved entities. The system uses regular telephone lines and operates on a computer-to-computer basis with the aid of standard formats and protocols. The information transmitted varies, depending on the preferences and needs of the participants, and may include sales data, advance shipping notices, inventory data, purchasing data, manufacturing data, and invoicing data.

Besides employing these two technologies, QR also requires the creation of smoothly operating partnership arrangements among the participants. This is a much more difficult task than acquiring bar coding and EDI technologies, as evidenced by the slow progress in this area.

Each participant has to assign to the partnership team suitable personnel from each relevant functional department, educate and train these people so they are familiar with the operation of each participant, train employees in bar coding and EDI, establish goals, agree on how to measure results, and make the necessary changes in the functional departments that are directly affected. Once established, the team must meet regularly, results must be monitored, and modifications must be made as needed.

Specific benefits derived from QR, in addition to those already mentioned, include an ability to put new products on the market more quickly in response to changing demand, faster order processing, real-time updating of inventory records, faster check outs at point of sale, faster communications, and improved relationships with customers and suppliers. Ultimately, QR translates into higher sales, lower costs, and greater profitability.

It should be noted that, to derive optimum benefits from QR, it is necessary to have in place a very flexible and responsive manufacturing process and to adopt several new methodologies, including, e.g., JIT and TQC. In addition, it is essential to acquire up-to-date materials-handling equipment and to introduce some of the other technologies reviewed in Chaps. 2 and 3.

The actual implementation of QR is still somewhat limited. At present, QR is mostly applied only to a number of selected product lines handled by each participating manufacturer and retailer. However, the methodology is spreading rapidly and should become the norm for most large retailers and their suppliers over the next several years.

In addition, manufacturers that do not cater directly to retail outlets also have begun to pay more attention to speeding up the distribution and delivery of their products to their customers. Their efforts in this area are known as Distribution Requirements Planning (DRP). These manufacturers cannot directly benefit from the detailed sales data feedback of QR, but they still must try to plan for quick changes in demand that affect their Manufacturing Resources Planning (MRP-II) and related programs. DRP is a component of sales and operation planning, a function that also includes market forecasting and distribution logistics.

5
Flexible and Cellular Manufacturing

This chapter covers two key concepts that are basic to factory automation: flexible and cellular manufacturing. It also includes a discussion of two types of arrangements to comprehensively update a manufacturing enterprise: flexible manufacturing systems and computer-integrated manufacturing.

This is followed by a discussion of the need for each manufacturing enterprise to carefully evaluate the applicability of automation in its particular circumstances. The last section deals with preventive maintenance, which is often overlooked and is becoming recognized as an essential function for today's manufacturing installation.

Flexible Manufacturing

Automated manufacturing contrasts with mechanized manufacturing. In the latter case, most of the physical effort is performed by machines, but human labor controls, guides, and participates in each operation. In a fully automated process, on the other hand, the direct involvement of human effort of any kind is much less.

Automated manufacturing includes both "hard" and "flexible" automation. Hard automation is exemplified by the well-known transfer line of dedicated equipment used in mass production but which has been upgraded by means of computerized controls.

As currently used, however, the term "automation" is usually intended to mean only flexible automation. The latter refers to a manufacturing process that adds "economy of scope" to "economy of scale." Economy of scope can be defined as having the flexibility to be able to produce a variety of products within the same family of products without having to make any changes in the process or the equipment.

In addition to being able to quickly adapt to changing volume requirements and changing product mixes, a truly flexible manufacturing installation also is able to accept new products, accommodate design specifications, cope with machine downtime, and—at least equally important—allow for expansion and reconfiguration so that a completely different line of products can be produced in a relatively short time.

Hard automation is generally faster than flexible automation and is still the preferred method for the mass production of uniform products. Although the acquisition cost of hard-automation equipment is lower than that of flexible-automation equipment, flexible equipment is cheaper in the long run if the production process has to be frequently modified or totally renewed.

In evaluating the need for flexibility, several criteria should be considered. A flexible manufacturing installation is usually preferable over a fixed, i.e., dedicated, installation if the life of the manufactured products is relatively short, there is a need for product customization, the production process continues to change, and/or market demand tends to fluctuate and is difficult to predict.

A typical updated manufacturing installation is likely to require a mix of hard- and flexible-automation equipment, with the optimum proportions depending on each company's unique circumstances. It never should be assumed that flexibility is always necessary or even helpful. Unwarranted flexibility and sophistication are likely to be counterproductive and not cost-effective; they will lower productivity and add to complexity and cost without providing any offsetting benefits.

It also should be noted that the human worker—still far more flexible than the most sophisticated robot today—is often able to outperform a flexible piece of equipment in many different applications. Therefore, the human worker should not be overlooked as a third possible option.

To justify the cost of a flexible system, its flexibility must be utilized to optimum advantage. Many U.S. manufacturers who have installed flexible automation fail to do so and, as a result, are disenchanted with their expensive installation. They tend to treat their automated processing equipment almost as if it were a transfer line. They make minimal product variations and concentrate on running the equipment at maximum capacity, instead of customizing their product and producing in small lots in response to market demand as a means of gaining a competitive advantage. Similarly, robotic assembly systems in the United States often are reprogrammed only a few times over the systems' lives—far below their intended frequency of up to several times per day.

The situation in the United States contrasts sharply with that in Japan. Japanese manufacturers utilize the flexibility of their systems far more effectively than U.S. manufacturers. They typically turn out several times as many different parts on their flexible equipment as their counterparts in the United States.

It appears that many U.S. manufacturers are not sufficiently knowledgeable about their own manufacturing processes, the proper application of flexible equipment, and the markets for their products to utilize their advanced equipment to optimum advantage. In addition, they have not taken the time and have not applied the considerable amount of effort that is required to carefully plan for the effective utilization of flexible automation.

To successfully implement flexible manufacturing, a company needs to make a number of changes in its engineering system support, organization, and employee attitudes. In addition, a serious effort must be made to simplify every aspect of the manufacturing process. Another prerequisite is the adoption of a Group Technology (GT) program.

Cellular Manufacturing

Usually the first basic piece of equipment with which to start the process of introducing automation into the manufacturing process is the CNC machine tool. It can be used in a stand-alone mode and can later be upgraded into a machining center by adding automatic tool-changing capability.

The next step involves changing the manufacturing process from a linear to a cellular layout. The cellular layout can be introduced at different levels of complexity, depending on the number of pieces of equipment involved and the extent of their linkage.

The simplest cellular arrangement is called a Flexible Manufacturing Cell (FMC). A plant equipped with Flexible Cellular Manufacturing (FCM) may have one or more FMCs.

The FMCs operate without any direct links to each other or to the rest of the manufacturing process. The cells usually consist of one or more CNC machine tools and a robot or other device for feeding the materials or parts to be processed, removing the output, and changing the tools as needed.

The staffing of individual cells varies considerably, depending on their sophistication. Nonautomated cells still benefit from some of the advantages of GT and a cellular layout. Fully automated cells operate with only minimal human supervision and are directed by a computer called a "cell controller."

Highly sophisticated, fully automated cells can run unattended on an almost continuous basis for three shifts. However, such cells are not commonly used, and they require a substantial amount of planning and debugging before they become fully operational.

FCM is most effective for small to medium lot-size batches of a family of parts that require similar processing, that may consist of somewhat dissimilar materials, and that may differ somewhat in shape and size. The cell has its own tools and is scheduled as a unit.

FCM is based on GT and is most effective when used in conjunction with other updating methodologies, such as Just-in-Time (JIT) and Total Quality Control (TQC). FCM also works best if a team approach to work assignments is used; this may include giving more authority and responsibility to the team and its members and rewarding the members, at least partly, on the basis of team results. It has been proven that the team approach provides the operators of a cellular-manufacturing installation with a greater sense of accomplishment and that this, in turn, tends to boost productivity.

As with most components of a successful updating program, sound planning is essential when changing over to flexible cellular manufacturing. This includes early involvement and thorough training of all employees, as well as planning for contingencies, such as changes in the product line, and allowing for future expansion and modification of each cell, e.g., by preparing a more elaborate foundation than is needed initially.

Flexible Manufacturing Systems

The second, somewhat more complex, flexible-automated manufacturing arrangement is called a Flexible Manufacturing System (FMS). An FMS consists of an integrated array of FMCs that are programmed, coordinated, and monitored by centralized computerized controls. The system is supported by an automated materials-handling system that delivers materials and parts, and removes processed parts in real time and in any sequence required by ongoing manufacturing operations.

An FMS is especially applicable for low-volume and midvolume manufacturers. The cost of an FMS can range between $2 million and $20 million, compared with as little as $400,000 for a single flexible manufacturing cell.

An FMS can be installed in only a part of a plant, or the FMS may occupy the whole plant building. Apart from the integrated linking of the FMCs in an FMS, the main difference between an FCM installation consisting of several cells and an FMS is one of complexity.

For most manufacturing companies, especially small and medium-sized ones, it is usually a good idea to start with installing one or more FMCs, rather than getting involved immediately with an FMS. FMCs offer many of the benefits of an FMS at much lower cost. FMCs provide a good introduction to flexible automation, are far more affordable, and can be the best solution for a company that only requires a limited degree of flexibility in its manufacturing process.

Also, in the case of a less sophisticated FMC that is staffed by humans, old equipment can often be utilized and reconfigured into a cellular layout to gain some of the benefits of cellular manufacturing at minimal expense, perhaps as an interim step toward greater sophistication later.

Improvements in FMS technology are continuing: Better diagnostics systems and sensors are being developed; equipment speeds are increasing; inspection systems are being upgraded, featuring on-line, noncontact methods; tool changing is becoming faster; and the number of manufacturing processes that can be automated is increasing.

Computer-Integrated Manufacturing

The third flexible-manufacturing system is called Computer-Integrated Manufacturing (CIM). The most advanced form of CIM is still largely anticipated. An installation employing a highly sophisticated CIM system is referred to as the fully automated factory or the "factory of the future."

CIM consists, in effect, of one or more FMSs that are totally integrated with each other and with the rest of the manufacturing enterprise by means of an all-encompassing system of computers. The computers control the complete enterprise with very limited human participation.

CIM is more than the sum total of its component technologies and methodologies. It represents a totally new approach to running a manufacturing enterprise. It involves every function and employee. In addition, it integrates every activity of a company—including the company's relationships with its customers and suppliers—by means of a computerized information and control system.

The adoption of CIM also requires the complete reorganization of a company's structure, the introduction of a new operational philosophy, and a new attitude on the part of the company's management and employees.

When installing an FMS, a variety of equipment that uses different communications codes can be connected, i.e., interfaced, by means of translating devices. In contrast, the goal of a true CIM installation is to completely *integrate* all components of the enterprise into a single, unified system without the use of any translating devices. Such components ideally are designed to work together harmoniously and to freely exchange information based on a single common code.

Unfortunately, for all practical purposes, such complete integration has not been achieved yet. There is an especially wide communications and compatibility gap between business systems (such as MRP-II) and manufacturing systems (CAD/CAM). In addition, many companies find it difficult to decide to adopt the radical changes in operational philosophy and practices that are required to make CIM effective. True CIM installations are still being perfected, and the number of even modest versions in existence today is very small.

It has been said that the installation of FCM systems and FMSs tends to create "islands of automation" that may hinder the eventual creation of a more comprehensive and more fully integrated system such as CIM. As emphasized elsewhere in this book, all *planning* for updating a manufacturing enterprise should be as comprehensive and farsighted as possible so as to facilitate any further upgrading that might become desirable in the future. On the other hand, the actual *implementation* of the plan can be completed in a number of separate steps spaced over a period of time.

If this principle is adhered to, each island of automation can be equipped with the proper "hookups" already in place and can have the proper characteristics, which will make it possible to easily integrate it with other components in the future.

Applicability of Automation

Not every manufacturing enterprise would benefit from maximum sophistication and integration of its component elements. In fact, most enterprises of modest size will probably be best served by only a limited degree of flexible automation and will at best have a need only for FCM or FMS, rather than CIM.

Although most small manufacturing enterprises are not likely to be candidates for CIM or even FMS, some of them will be able to raise their productivity by acquiring a Computer-Aided Design (CAD) system and/or installing a single FMC. It is interesting to note in this connection that very small machine shops have been using the nonautomated equivalent of FCM without realizing it. Since these shops usually do not have more than one machine of the same general type, they have not been subjected to the temptation of organizing their equipment into functional groupings. Thus, when introducing automation in such shops, the layout does not have to be reorganized.

This still leaves a large majority of small manufacturing companies that have no need for any kind of highly sophisticated automation equipment. However, most of these companies still can benefit greatly from adopting some of the other methodologies reviewed in Chap. 4.

Especially helpful in this respect is process simplification, a systematic effort to eliminate all unnecessary complexity, which is discussed in some detail in Chap. 14. It has been estimated that, in some cases, process simplification alone can provide up to 75 percent of the total improvement to be expected from a comprehensive updating program at only a small fraction of the cost.

In conclusion, it should be emphasized that a complete updating program may consist of at least three different basic components: methodologies, technologies, and computerization. These components can be applied in varying combinations as needed.

The introduction of automation technology into a manufacturing company requires computerization, but the reverse is not true: Often computerized information and control systems can be very effective in improving the productivity of certain nonautomated activities and processes. Similarly, while automation requires the introduction of most of the methodologies described in this chapter, several of the methodologies can be utilized to advantage without acquiring any automation equipment or even getting involved in extensive computerization.

Each company must carefully assess its needs, conduct a cost/benefit analysis, and then decide on the extent of updating and the mix of the three basic components that are most appropriate for its unique circumstances.

Preventive Maintenance

As manufacturing companies install more and more sophisticated equipment and software and increase their reliance on uninterrupted trouble-free functioning of all components of their operation, the maintenance function becomes critically important. Reasons for the increasing importance of maintenance include:

- The updated, automated installation will be running more like a continuous-process plant, and therefore the equipment must be constantly available and reliable.

- An automated plant is more equipment intensive, and its equipment is more complex and costly.

- There are fewer operators to watch for malfunctions.

- There is more reliance on computers and less on humans to operate the machines.

Areas that require maintenance can be classified into four types: computers, automated equipment, related software, and the utilities and other supporting elements that service the automated equipment. Manufacturers' and vendors' warranties cover most of the equipment they sell for a limited period of time. Whenever available, annual maintenance contracts are frequently purchased to guarantee outside service and assistance beyond the warranty period. As the price of computers has continued to decline and their reliability has improved, computer users have tended to cut back on maintenance contracts for computers, especially personal computers.

As regards automation equipment other than computers, the user of this equipment generally bears full responsibility for its proper maintenance. Such responsibility should be shifted as much as possible to the operators and controllers of each individual piece of equipment. They must be trained in detecting and correcting minor malfunctionings and call on maintenance and repair specialists only when needed.

For several reasons, it is advisable to have such specialists available in-house. Not only is speed of the utmost importance for a manufacturing company that utilizes time-based methodologies, but a technically sophisticated manufacturer cannot afford to rely exclusively on outside vendor assistance—even if such assistance is outstanding. Outside assistance should normally be utilized only as a supplementary backup for the user's own maintenance and repair staff.

The maintenance function itself is undergoing significant change. Maintenance originally was usually limited to such simple tasks as periodic lubrication, and repairs were undertaken when the equipment malfunctioned.

However, today it is becoming increasingly important to minimize costly repairs to the sophisticated equipment that is being installed and to avoid lengthy disruptive downtime of the manufacturing process. This means that the emphasis must be shifted from taking corrective measures to anticipating and quickly analyzing potential problems and to prevent as much as possible any problems from occurring in the first place.

This new approach to maintenance, called Preventive Maintenance (PM), requires the preparation and conscientious implementation of a comprehensive program with detailed schedules and assignments covering each piece of equipment. For most installations, such PM programs should be computerized. The software can be entirely developed in-house, or a software package can be purchased; the software will normally need some customization.

PM is becoming increasingly sophisticated. Going beyond basic PM, some companies are beginning to practice what is called "predictive maintenance." This method employs advanced predictive techniques such as automated internal diagnostics and vibration sensors, as well as keeping detailed repair records for each piece of equipment.

Another useful aid for improving PM is the application of artificial intelligence techniques. Expert systems have been developed that not only facilitate the diagnosis of complex problems by specialists but also enable regular shop floor personnel to troubleshoot simple problems.

All of this is being done in an effort to anticipate when a particular machine is likely to malfunction well before it actually happens. By replacing or repairing equipment that appears ready for a breakdown, repair costs and unscheduled downtime can be further minimized. Other benefits of an effective, advanced PM program include lower inventories of spare parts, lower overall maintenance costs, improved operational control, and prolonged service life of plant and equipment.

Basic computerized programs can increase uptime to between 70 and 80 percent, while more sophisticated programs can achieve 80 to 90 percent uptime. This compares with only 50 to 60 percent uptime for manual PM programs.

A computerized PM program can save a company as much as one-third of its annual repair and maintenance costs. This is especially worthwhile since the cost of the repair and maintenance of high-technology equipment may reach well above 20 percent of the total manufacturing cost. An effective PM program usually pays for itself within 2 years, and often within 1 year.

The successful introduction of a PM program requires adopting a totally new approach to maintenance on the part of everyone concerned. Some of the specific steps to be taken include:

- Training the equipment operators to become responsible for initial (first-aid) maintenance

- Selecting equipment that is more trouble-free
- Correcting equipment weaknesses as they become apparent
- Keeping records of maintenance problems of each piece of equipment and its components, including life-cycle costs

Most continuous-process plants already employ sophisticated maintenance procedures and find it cost-effective to pay for the accompanying redundancy, fault tolerance, diagnostics, and service contracts. However, surveys indicate that, although many general managers of other types of manufacturing installations are becoming increasingly aware of the need for PM, a large majority of such plants still practice old-style corrective maintenance and do not have an adequate PM program in place.

6
Progress Made and Outlook

Historical Background

Flexible, computer-aided factory automation is only a few decades old. Acceptance of the new technologies and methodologies did not begin to take hold until the late 1970s.

The following are some of the prominent early developments that led to the current phase of automation and factory modernization:

- The first modern computer was created in 1946 and became commercially available in 1951; minicomputers and microcomputers appeared in the late 1960s; and workstations were introduced around 1980.

- The first numerically controlled machine tool was developed in the early 1950s, and such machine tools became commercially available in the 1960s.

- The robot was invented in 1946. Robots started to be commercially produced in 1959, and the first industrial robot to be used in a production process was installed in 1962. Robots began to play a major role in manufacturing in the late 1970s.

- Automated Storage and Retrieval Systems (AS/RSs) originated in the 1950s.

- The principles of Total Quality Control (TQC) were first spelled out in 1961, but were not applied much in the United States until the 1970s.

- Bar coding was first used in 1965 for tracking railroad cars.

- The first Flexible Manufacturing System (FMS) was constructed in the mid-1960s and installed in a machine shop as "System 24." The system could operate 24 hours a day, of which 16 hours were totally unstaffed. However, the concept for such a system remained mostly of only academic interest until the early 1980s when a number of systems were installed. By the late 1980s, Flexible Manufacturing Cells began to be favored over FMSs as more appropriate for many manufacturing operations, at least as an initial step that might be followed up later by installing a more complex system.

- The Programmable Logic Controller (PLC) was invented in 1969 as a replacement for the hard-wired relay board. The integrated controller, combining the functions and capabilities of a PLC and a Distributed Control System (DCS), made its appearance only in the late 1980s.

- The first Electronic Data Interchange (EDI) systems were used in the trucking industry around 1970; they spread to the automotive and retailing sectors during the 1970s and started to become widely accepted in the mid-1980s.

- The term Computer-Integrated Manufacturing (CIM) was coined in 1974, and became widely used after 1980.

- Computerized maintenance systems were introduced in the 1970s.

- Machine vision became a viable technology for use in automated manufacturing about 1980.

- The just-in-time methodology was introduced in Japan around 1970 but did not gain acceptance in the United States until 1980.

- Process planning was done manually until the 1960s. Computer-Assisted Process Planning (CAPP) developed gradually over the next two decades, and Expert Systems (ESs) began to be utilized in process planning during the 1980s.

Current Status

Statistical information on the size of the automation market tends to be spotty and unreliable. Problems in measuring its size include a lack of agreement as to what exactly constitutes factory automation and which components should be included, as well as the absence of a factory-automation category among the various types of data collected by the federal government.

In fact, there is as yet no such entity as a single factory-automation market. The market is fragmented and consists of a large number of separate segments. Some of these segments are reported statistically on a regular basis, while no such standardized information is available for other segments.

There are at least five segments that are frequently included when estimating the total factory-automation market: factory computers, machine tools and controls, automated materials-handling equipment, Computer-Aided Design and Computer-Aided Manufacturing (CAD/CAM), and robots.

Other segments for which estimates are sometimes provided include process controllers, sensors, actuators, and automated-inspection and -testing equipment. Estimates are rare for spending on such automation services as design, planning, project management, assembly, start-up, and training.

During the first half of the 1980s, a number of very large U.S. manufacturing companies took the lead in extensively automating some of their operations and established state-of-the-art showplaces at great expense. Since they were pioneers, it is only natural that they encountered many serious obstacles and frustrations and that some of these installations did not perform as expected. However, many lessons were learned that should be helpful in making further progress in implementing the new technologies.

Until recently, the vast majority of U.S. manufacturers—especially companies with fewer than fifty employees, which form the mainstay of the U.S. manufacturing sector—had refrained from following the example of the large pioneering companies. This situation has begun to change: Factory automation no longer is the exclusive domain of a few very large companies.

Smaller companies have become interested in updating their enterprise. They are adopting the new technologies and methodologies—many of which are now available in packaged form—on a gradual, incremental basis, as warranted by their individual circumstances and permitted by their financial resources. These smaller companies tend to rely more on outside assistance both in planning and implementing their updating programs. Even so, very large companies are still far more likely to have advanced manufacturing equipment in place than very small companies.

The main impetus for pursuing an updating program is competitive pressure from abroad. This means that companies heavily involved in exports or in producing items that face aggressively priced imports are particularly apt to investigate possibilities for modernizing their operations.

The current phase of factory automation and modernization is characterized by conservatism and caution. Often this means less sophisticated installations that more directly reflect specific needs and less emphasis on what is technologically possible.

On the average, investment by manufacturing companies in automation still represents only a small fraction of their total investment expenditures—probably less than 20 percent. Only a relatively small number of manufacturers are totally committed to achieve both high speed and high flexibility in their operations by means of a comprehensive, sophisticated automated installation.

Computer-integrated manufacturing—presumably the ultimate phase of the current modernization effort—remains an elusive concept, still difficult to achieve. In fact, CIM is not appropriate for many manufacturing organizations.

However, various surveys indicate that a sizable portion of all manufacturing companies have already adopted at least some of the components of an updating program discussed in this book. The automotive sector has taken the lead, followed by electronics, aircraft, and food processing.

Technologies and methodologies that are among the first to be implemented include Computer-Aided Design (CAD), numerical control of machine tools, automated data collection, electronic data interchange, Just-in-Time (JIT), and Manufacturing Resources Planning (MRP-II). Very large manufacturing companies tend to additionally favor total quality control and Flexible Manufacturing Cells (FMCs) and FMSs.

Reportedly, about one-half of all manufacturing plants with 500 employees or more are utilizing at least some flexible manufacturing equipment. This includes FMCs and FMSs, as well as automated-machining centers.

Industrial computers and controllers, i.e., computers used on the factory floor, have become well entrenched. In recent years workstations have been the fastest growing type of computer in manufacturing companies. Workstations were first used mainly in the design function, but are increasingly being used on the factory floor also.

CAD and Computer-Aided Engineering (CAE) systems have come into widespread use, while Computer-Aided Manufacturing (CAM) has lagged somewhat. However, in recent years, CAM has begun to be applied more widely. Even so, only a small fraction of all manufacturing companies are currently using CAD to directly program numerically controlled machine tools. Also, although three-dimensional design systems are available, most engineers still use two-dimensional systems to actually design new products.

Investment in robots still represents only a small portion of total spending on automated equipment. About 4500 new robots are being installed annually, of which about one-half are in the automotive sector. At the end of 1990, the robot population in the United States totaled about 40,000 units, compared with only 5000 units a decade earlier.

Well over one-third of all manufacturing companies make at least some use of Automatic Identification (Auto.ID) technologies. About three-fourths of all systems that are being installed annually utilize bar coding.

The use of electronic data interchange has been growing rapidly, especially among very large manufacturers. Just-in-time has been accepted—at least as a worthwhile goal to be pursued seriously—by more than one-half the total number of manufacturing companies. Although the use of sophisticated MRP-II systems is still rather limited, about one-third the total number of manufacturing companies have reportedly installed at least a modest version of such systems.

Total quality control has been adopted as a basic guiding principle by a large majority of very large manufacturing companies and also by many smaller companies. Many very large companies also have become interested in Artificial Intelligence (AI) and have acquired one or more expert systems. At the end of 1990, about 1800 AS/RSs had been installed, mostly by very large manufacturing companies and the federal government.

Several other technologies and methodologies have not been applied very widely in the manufacturing sector thus far. As already mentioned in Chap. 3, sophisticated computer-aided process planning systems are employed by a relatively small number of manufacturing companies; in most companies the task of process planning is still performed manually by highly experienced manufacturing engineers.

Similarly, Automated Guided Vehicles (AGVs) are used by only a few percent of all manufacturing companies, often in direct support of AS/RSs as an aid to achieving JIT. One-half the total number of such vehicles have been installed by very large firms, with automotive companies accounting for one-fourth of the total.

When comparing the use of advanced manufacturing technology in the United States with that abroad, the United States appears to be lagging badly in most areas behind Japan, Germany, and several other countries in western Europe. Notable exceptions are in the use of computers, computer software, and CAD. In some areas, such as robotics, the United States also still has the lead in innovation but fails to aggressively utilize its superior know-how.

It has been estimated that, at the end of 1990, Japan and Germany each had about twice as many FMSs installed as the United States—after allowing for the difference in size of the three countries. The United States' lag in the use of robots is even larger. Relative to its size, Japan annually installs about six times as many robots as the United States— even after adjusting the number of robots in Japan for that country's much broader definition of a robot. The United States also trails Sweden, Germany, and Italy in robot use.

Japan is an avid believer in the cost-effectiveness of AGVs. It annually installs about 20 times as many units as the United States, relative to its size, while western Europe as a whole installs about 6 times as many AGVs as the United States. Japan also is well ahead in the number of AS/RSs it installs annually—about six times as many as the United States, again on a relative basis—and so is western Europe.

Outlook

The use of FMCs and—to a lesser extent—FMSs is expected to grow more rapidly during the 1990s than during the past decade. They will be installed not only by large companies but also increasingly by small and midsize companies. However, flexible-automated equipment will be more carefully evaluated on its merits and will be intermixed with the use of human workers wherever appropriate.

Robots, similarly, will gain recognition as valuable tools in applications where they can be especially effective. It is anticipated that the number of robots installed in the United States will exceed 100,000 by the year 2000, compared with 40,000 in 1990.

Auto.ID, combined with EDI, will likely become one of the fastest growing technologies during the current decade. The number of manufacturing companies that use Auto.ID in 1997 is expected to be at least twice the number in 1992. Bar coding will continue to be the most widely used data collection technology and will become more sophisticated. Bar codes will increasingly be used as "portable data bases," i.e., they will be able to carry more information by means of two-dimensional code symbology. In addition, bar-code scanners will be improved so that they will be able to read damaged symbols.

The installation of EDI equipment is likely to continue at a very rapid rate. Eventually, a large majority of manufacturing companies for which this technology is appropriate will utilize it. EDI is expected to be integrated more fully with Auto.ID.

The sale of artificial intelligence equipment and software will probably increase significantly during the 1990s. More than one-half the number of large manufacturing companies will soon have installed one or more ESs. Automated equipment will increasingly feature some embedded AI capability. Fuzzy logic will follow on the heels of ES, but other applications of neural networks will take a while longer before becoming commercially available for use in manufacturing.

Sophisticated Preventive Maintenance (PM) systems are likely to be viewed more and more as another essential component of a TQC program. They will incorporate ES and utilize self-diagnostic capabilities built into the automated equipment. In addition, they will be more closely integrated with the functioning of the manufacturing operation, partly by directly interfacing with MRP-II.

Computers will continue to undergo numerous changes—in sophistication as well as in application—and will invade the factory floor in ever larger numbers. The trend to microcomputers is expected to intensify, and such computers are likely to be mass-produced as nonproprietary products by fewer manufacturers. It is anticipated that computers will increasingly feature parallel processing and Reduced-Instruction-Set Computing (RISC), and be run on Object-Oriented Programming Systems (OOPS).

Computers also will become even more user friendly, and, as a result, fewer highly skilled programmers will be required. Communication between the computer and its user will be further facilitated by voice input—thus, reducing the need for keyboarding information—head-mounted displays, and other new devices. An ever larger variety of packaged software programs with embedded programming tools will become available.

For the time being, achieving the ideal of totally "open" systems will remain elusive. However, further progress toward computer compatibility and connectivity can be expected. UNIX and Manufacturing Automation Protocol (MAP) are likely to become more widely adopted, and more software programs that facilitate the connectivity of incompatible systems will become available. So-called software enablers, i.e., programs that standardize the interfaces of applications programs, will help.

The updating programs that are going to be implemented over the years ahead are going to be more "mature" than earlier efforts. They will benefit from some of the lessons learned by companies that pioneered the new technologies and methodologies, including:

- Well-thought-out comprehensive and detailed planning will precede any effort to update a manufacturing enterprise.
- Overly ambitious comprehensive CIM programs that the company is not equipped to handle will be avoided.

- Careful consideration will be given to evaluating the cost-effectiveness of automation in each specific proposed application, and human workers will be retained wherever it is appropriate.

- Computerization of information and communications as well as the introduction of some of the new methodologies will receive more consideration, at least initially, than the installation of highly sophisticated automated equipment.

- Special attention will be paid to employee involvement and training, simplification of the existing manufacturing process, efforts to make continuous incremental improvements, and decentralization of the organizational structure.

As regards the overall outlook for bringing U.S. manufacturing up-to-date, there are indications that interest in applying the technologies and methodologies described in this book among not only large manufacturing companies but also many smaller companies is finally increasing. The main driving force that will be responsible for this interest will continue to be competitive pressures, especially from abroad.

The unanswered question at this time is whether the U.S. manufacturing sector as a whole will proceed quickly enough to avoid further serious losses to its competitive position in the world market. Progress thus far has been disappointingly slow, and it is to be hoped that the pace of modernization will soon pick up significantly. However, regardless of the speed or lack of speed with which the U.S. manufacturing sector is going to update itself in the current decade, each company can and must make its own decision regarding its course of action.

The decision whether or not to initiate a comprehensive updating program depends heavily on the individual circumstances of each company. They include the type of products it manufactures, the likely cost-effectiveness of such a program, the extent of foreign and domestic competition it faces, the degree of farsightedness of its top executives, its exposure to some of the new approaches to manufacturing, and its financial resources.

7

Planning Basics

As is the case with any complex task involving the introduction of major changes, proper planning is a key requirement for a successful program for updating a manufacturing enterprise. However, since the changes to be brought about are often so encompassing and far-reaching, affecting all functions of a typical manufacturing operation, and since these changes could well determine the future success or failure of the enterprise, planning will have to be taken much more seriously than is usually the case in most manufacturing firms.

To lay the proper foundation for the actual planning process of updating the organization, many companies may find it helpful to first evaluate and, if necessary, improve their present short- and long-term planning process. Each company will require its own individual variety of planning procedures, depending on such factors as the type, size, and complexity of the organization, and the personal preferences of its general management.

Executives who feel that the planning process in their own company requires considerable strengthening will benefit from the material presented in this chapter on the basics of planning in general. Planning the actual updating process is dealt with in Chap. 8.

Definition and Role of Planning

What Is Planning?

Planning can be defined simply as a method for attempting to make things happen that would not occur without it. It is a technique for establishing and maintaining a sense of *direction*.

The planning process is complex and time-consuming. It requires clear thinking and sound analysis.

The purpose of planning is to initiate a set of actions that are most likely to result in the optimal achievement of specified objectives over a period of time. Effective planning can be described as a *continuing* process, involving:

- Establishing objectives and numerical targets
- Monitoring current position
- Monitoring the environment
- Anticipating changes in the environment
- Deciding on a set of actions to be taken that are likely to lead to the desired result
- Implementing each of these actions in accordance with a certain time frame

The first and most important step in the process is establishing objectives on the basis of sound judgment. If the judgment is bad, a good plan can only help an organization to reach the wrong target in an efficient manner.

The last step in the process is the formulation of an action program that will transform the plan into actuality. Without this last step, a plan remains a theoretical exercise.

Since a plan is intended to achieve something that would not be accomplished without it, in theory, there is no need for a plan if a company's future performance is expected to conform to the desired goals. However, in practice that is not likely to ever be the case for at least two reasons:

1. Management is not apt to be content with a simple extrapolation of current business volume and profits over the next few years.
2. External and internal changes are likely to occur that will cause adverse changes in the company's business *unless* certain actions are taken.

In both cases, a plan is indispensable in trying to achieve the company's objectives. In fact, a carefully prepared and implemented business plan is as essential for managing a successful, large business enterprise as a set of engineering drawings is for building a sound, large physical structure.

In preparing a plan, it is important to realize that the object is not necessarily to establish a *straight* path to a certain goal. This is a misunderstanding that leads to frustration and is responsible for a lot of disenchantment with planning.

Instead, planning is akin to navigating a ship: A plan represents a course that is charted at a point in time but that is seldom, if ever, followed exactly as drawn. Almost from the moment its course has been charted, the ship will begin to deviate from its planned course as a result of changes in the various forces that affect it.

Yet, no one will claim that, therefore, it is useless to chart a ship's course. Instead, the process of determining the present location, anticipating the current and wind, charting a new course, and taking corrective action is repeated at intervals until the destination is reached. This analogy points up the importance of careful monitoring, frequent feedback, and adequate flexibility to continue to take the necessary actions to stay on course.

Planning is one of the most important functions of a manager. The more general his or her responsibilities are, the more time the manager should devote to planning, and the longer his or her time-span should be.

Top general management occupies the top level in the planning hierarchy. The attitude of top management toward planning determines the degree of acceptance of planning throughout the organization and the degree of effectiveness of the planning process.

How Much Planning Is Needed?

Since it is clear that planning is necessary, the next question is: How much should a company plan? There are at least four different approaches to planning:

- Informal, undocumented planning—useful mainly for very small companies
- Problem-oriented planning, concentrating on specific problems and how to solve them—useful mainly for short-term emergency situations
- Planning by exception, concentrating on what needs to be done differently to achieve the objectives—some of this can be helpful in reducing the amount of planning detail, but it cannot be substituted for a complete plan
- Comprehensive planning by means of a set of formal plan documents covering all aspects of a company's operations

Generally speaking, the larger and more complex an organization is, the more it needs to have a detailed, formal plan.

One of the most difficult challenges in a large, complex organization is to ensure effective, harmonious coordination and collaboration of all units in striving for the achievement of the company's goals. A well thought-out, comprehensive plan is an indispensable tool for accomplishing this.

Benefits and Requirements

Benefits of Planning

The benefits of preparing a plan extend well beyond the plan's primary usefulness as a tool for reaching the company's objectives. In fact, even if a plan is not implemented or monitored in any systematic fashion, it is still likely to be worthwhile to go through the planning exercise.

Included among the different benefits of preparing a plan are the following:

- Serves as a program and a schedule for performing specific tasks
- Facilitates monitoring progress toward achieving the stated objectives and targets
- Helps management to respond more quickly to any sudden need for changes in targets or operations
- Helps to inform other units of the organization about what each unit intends to do during the plan year
- Helps to coordinate the activities of all units of the organization
- Tends to show up unfilled needs, duplication of efforts, and inefficiencies
- Helps to ensure that the objectives and targets of each unit are realistic
- Provides a check on whether the sum total of the plans of all the units is likely to result in the accomplishment of the overall objectives and targets established by top general management

In addition to the above, the planning *process*—as contrasted with the plan itself—also provides the following benefits:

- Forces each contributor to the plan to think ahead about his or her work during the plan year

- Stimulates creative thinking by top management about the company's expansion and profitability, and about the future of the company generally

- Helps top management cope more effectively with any unforeseen developments that require quick countermeasures because management has become more aware of the possible impact of such events and has gained experience in preparing a plan of action to meet such challenges

Planning Requirements

Since planning is intended to result in change and involves control and accountability, all of which tend to be resisted to some extent, carefully *planning the planning process* is important for paving the way. In addition, care should be taken to avoid a number of other pitfalls that could easily prevent planning from becoming an effective tool for guiding the future of an organization.

The following are among the requirements for a successful plan:

- The overall objectives and targets adopted by top general management should be *realistic* and *specific.*

- The plan should be *useful* and *usable,* i.e., it should contain a program that has practical value and that is capable of being implemented.

- The various plans, short-term, long-term, budget, etc., should be adequately *tied in* with each other.

- Top general management should make it clear that it is wholeheartedly *committed to planning* generally and to the preparation and implementation of a plan.

- This commitment should be *expressed in* such *tangible forms* as periodic communications with the plan's contributors before, during, and after the plan preparation period; unstinting participation in the plan preparation as appropriate; and perhaps the establishment of a bonus system linked to the plan's implementation.

- In addition, top general management should make it clear that planning is as important as production and that each contributor is expected to *allocate* adequate *time* to the preparation of his or her segment of the plan.

- The contributors should be given an adequate *understanding* of the plan's purpose and use and should be *trained* in the methodology of preparing a plan.

- The planning process should be *directed and coordinated by a planning executive.* This individual should also be responsible for editing the drafts and integrating the various plan segments into a single corporate summary plan.

- In preparing the plan, the necessary *basic information* concerning the outlook for the economic environment and for each market should be collected by each contributor and/or made available to him or her by a central staff office.

- The preparation of the plan segment of each unit of the company should be *coordinated* with that of the other units.

- The plan, including the numerical targets and the action program, should be prepared by means of *interaction* among the various layers of management, i.e., an interactive process combining bottom-up and top-down planning.

- Each contributor at the implementation level should be asked for a *commitment to implement* the plan for his or her unit.

- The implementation of the plan should be *monitored* on a regular basis.

- The plan should be *revised,* either periodically or as needed, to keep it current and meaningful.

Some of these requirements are discussed in more detail in the sections below.

Since planning is a complex procedure involving a large number of individuals, it usually takes several annual planning cycles before a workable system is in place.

Types of Plans

Short-term planning usually covers a period of 1 year (sometimes 2), while long-term planning typically deals with a period of 5 to 10 years ahead. The 1-year plan must be based on the long-term objectives and targets of an organization; these are usually embodied in a long-term plan that is strategic in nature and points out the direction in which each 1-year plan should be aimed. In addition, the 1-year plan should be coordinated with the budget and the financial plan.

For most types of organizations, marketing is one of the key topics of a 1-year plan. In some cases, it is preferable to split the 1-year plan into two separate plans: a sales plan and a business plan. The sales plan serves as an action plan for the marketing and sales function, while the business plan covers all other topics of the 1-year plan.

Both plans have to be closely interrelated and prepared simultaneously. The preliminary targets in the business plan must be checked against the preliminary action program outlined in the sales plan, and vice versa, before they are finalized.

The preparation of the sales plan, business plan, and long-term strategic plan requires the participation and close cooperation of all layers of management by means of an iterative feedback process. The objectives and the targets are initiated top-down, while the action program is initiated bottom-up.

The sales plan is prepared mainly bottom-up and the strategic plan is prepared mainly top-down. The business plan requires a balanced combination of top-down and bottom-up interaction.

Many companies beyond a certain size have found it necessary to establish a planning office that is responsible for directing and coordinating the planning process, and for providing staff support for the line managers who do the actual planning itself. The manager of such a function should report to someone at the top general management level.

The usual responsibilities of the various layers of management for the plan preparation process can be summarized as follows (this can be modified according to circumstances and personal preferences):

Top general management
- Establish the broad objectives, strategies, and overall targets of the strategic plan
- Approve the business plan and the strategic plan
- Monitor the implementation of the strategic plan[1]

Other top management
- Determine the specific targets and action program of the strategic plan
- Participate in the preparation of the business plan
- Consult on the sales plan
- Approve the sales plan
- Monitor the implementation of the business plan

---

[1]A suggested monitoring frequency is annually for the strategic plan, semiannually for the business plan, and quarterly for the sales plan.

Middle-line management

- Participate in the preparation of the business plan
- Prepare most of the sales plan
- Monitor the implementation of the sales plan

Planning and marketing staff management[2]

- Prepare information on the economic outlook
- Prepare information on each of the company's markets as needed
- Participate in the preparation of numerical targets
- Direct and coordinate the planning process, edit the plan segments, and prepare corporate summaries of the plans

Plan Contents

The process of preparing a plan that will contribute to shaping the future of an organization requires the harmonious collaboration of a large number of managers who are able and willing to devote considerable effort and sound analysis to this task.

Especially in large and complex organizations, the planning effort requires strong central direction with full support from top general management. Included in such direction should be the distribution of a set of specific instructions for preparing the plan as well as basic information concerning assumptions, overall objectives, etc., that will be needed by the contributors to the plan.

As a general rule, plans should be kept as brief and succinct as possible and should include only material that is directly relevant to the plan. Thus, information about the responsibilities of each unit, organizational details, descriptions of markets, etc., should be omitted, *except for changes* that have a bearing on the plan.

In addition, details of the action program that are of concern only to a limited number of people should be summarized in the plan. The details themselves should be added as an appendix or issued as a separate document.

A typical 1-year business plan deals with four basic topics:

1. An evaluation of the present and recent past, including a comparison of actual performance with planned performance
2. A projection of the present into the future without any plan

---

[2]Each task applies to all three types of plans.

3. Desired objectives and targets

4. An action program designed to cause future performance to exceed the projection and approximate the target

The second basic topic is discussed in some detail in the two sections that follow.

Targets versus Projections

Since a plan is intended to achieve something that would probably not be achieved without it, management should first determine what would happen in the absence of a plan.

Such a "projection" of the momentum of a company—for the coming year and for the next 5 years—requires a statistical exercise that takes into account such factors as historical trend of the sales volume, past and anticipated changes in the economic environment, the outlook for specific markets for the company's products, and anticipated changes within the company.

After such a projection has been prepared, management can evaluate the reasonableness of the various proposed targets and decide whether it is possible and desirable to try to close up the gap between the projected business volume and the targeted business volume by taking a set of actions. If the resources required to undertake these actions are not available, or if it is decided that their cost is too high, top management will have to lower the proposed targets.

Although the process of preparing projections involves making many assumptions, it *does* provide a benchmark for evaluating the reasonableness of the proposed targets. Without such projections, the establishment of targets tends to be a matter of personal judgment based on implicit assumptions and, therefore, is even less accurate than the projection method.

Assumptions

Assumptions, whether implicit or explicit, about the outlook for the economic environment and each of the company's markets play an important role in making projections and establishing numerical targets. Since implicit assumptions are difficult to deal with and each contributor is apt to have his or her own set of assumptions that may differ radically from those of the other contributors, it is advisable to state all the assumptions in the plan.

Some of the information necessary for the formulation of assumptions could be gathered and analyzed by the contributors themselves, especially information concerning the local economy and narrow market segments with which they are personally acquainted. The remainder of the necessary information that cannot be readily obtained and/or analyzed by the contributors should be provided by a central planning or marketing staff office.

Since assumptions sometimes prove to be wrong and since unforeseen developments can play havoc with the implementation of a plan, management should formulate a range of assumptions and several scenarios, and prepare a corresponding set of contingency plans. However, contingency planning is a sophisticated process that may not be possible at an early stage in the evolution of the planning process. In addition, contingency planning may not even be necessary for certain companies, depending on their circumstances and the inclinations of top general management. Often it will be sufficient to prepare a single plan, watch for unanticipated changes, and make adjustments in the plan as required.

Follow-up

Two of the principal prerequisites for ensuring that a plan is implemented and remains meaningful are proper monitoring and timely revisions. Each segment of the action program should be monitored on a regular basis. In addition, it is necessary to closely watch for changes in the external environment as well as in the organization itself that may affect the assumptions and achieving the objectives and targets.

It is especially helpful in the case of the sales plan to hold quarterly meetings. The progress that has been made during the previous quarter should be reviewed, and the plan should be updated by adding more details concerning specific assignments for the action program of the next quarter.

A process for updating and revising the plan as needed should be linked with the monitoring process. Unless the required changes are made promptly, the plan tends to lose credibility and become a meaningless document.

Improving the Planning Process

Planning is a continuous function, not just a once-a-year exercise. It should rate top priority on a manager's list of responsibilities as an essential and effective method for safeguarding and improving the company's profitability.

However, in many companies, planning is typically regarded—especially by middle managers—at best as a nonincome-producing overhead activity, a necessary evil. At worst planning is viewed as a total waste of time, an unnecessary exercise in which participation should be limited or shirked as much as possible.

Since the effectiveness of planning depends on the full cooperation of everyone who has to make a contribution and requires all contributors to have some minimal skills in this activity, top management may find it worthwhile to take several steps to promote a better understanding of planning and improve participation. Some of these steps, as well as other actions that may help upgrade the planning process, are outlined below.

A Separate Planning Function

If a company does not already have a separate planning function in place, top management may want to consider establishing such a function. Its responsibilities should include directing and coordinating the preparation of the various plans, editing the drafts, consolidating the plans of each business unit into a single set of company plans, and coordinating the monitoring and revision processes.

Incentives

To impress upon everyone the importance top management attaches to planning, the performance rating system for managers could be modified to include each manager's effectiveness in short- and long-term planning as an additional factor. Furthermore, a bonus system could be established that would be based at least partly on a qualitative evaluation of each manager's success in implementing his or her portion of the action program of the company's plan.

Training

A series of presentations should be made by one or more top managers to explain the purpose, impact, and importance of the company's various types of plans. If more guidance is needed, training could be provided in how to prepare plans, including the collection of information, the evaluation of market prospects, the process of linking specific actions to the targets, and vertical and horizontal coordination with other managers.

Coordination

Regular horizontal coordination meetings should be held, as needed during the annual planning cycle, of selected appropriate groups of contributors to the plans, e.g., of all the divisional managers or office managers. Similarly, regular meetings should be scheduled of certain executives at different levels to promote vertical coordination of the plans.

Information

Each unit of the company should be provided with explicit guidelines concerning its short-term goals and its long-term mission. The guidelines should be in accordance with the overall objectives stated in the strategic plan.

If it is appropriate, the company's market research program could be expanded to include at least a brief review of each current and potential market for the company's products.

If it is relevant to the company's business, a study could be made to analyze the extent to which, and the manner in which, the company's sales volume and its components are influenced by developments in the national and regional economy.

Finally, if the results of such a study warrant, information about present and anticipated outside developments should be incorporated into the assumptions that are provided to the plan's contributors. This information should serve as a basis for calculating numerical targets for the contributors' particular area of responsibility.

Plan Distribution and Analysis

Everyone in the organization who is involved in plan preparation and implementation should receive a copy of each completed plan. Also, the completed plans and their impacts should be discussed at meetings with all the managers directly involved in their implementation. Periodic follow-up meetings should be held to review the results of monitoring the implementation and revision processes.

Ultimately, the importance of planning in an organization as perceived by most managers—and thereby its effectiveness—will depend heavily on the example set by top management. Top management must consistently utilize planning themselves, request planning input from all levels and functions within the organization, and continually measure and reward actual performance against the plan.

8

Preparing the Updating Program

This chapter first reviews the role of strategic planning as a prerequisite for a successful updating program. Next, five steps are outlined that must be taken as part of the process of preparing the program. This is followed by a discussion of simulation as a cost-effective tool to simplify the planning process and assure that the planned installation will perform as expected. The last section deals with the selection, composition, and function of the planning team that will be responsible for planning and implementing the updating program.

A comprehensive updating program is apt to include a large variety of new technologies and methodologies, many of which have been dealt with in Chaps. 2 through 5. Most of these technologies and methodologies interact with each other and usually are dependent on each other for their proper implementation. It is necessary, therefore, to take into account these interactions and dependencies and make sure that the planned components fit together harmoniously and form a workable and effective program.

Need for Strategic Planning

If ever there is a need for strategic planning, it is when contemplating the updating and possible automation of a manufacturing enterprise. In fact, it can be stated that strategic planning is an absolute prerequisite for successful automation.

Many manufacturing executives apparently have come to agree that strategic planning is of vital importance for their companies' continued success. Although most have tended to be preoccupied with "fire fighting" and short-term objectives, they now seem to be willing to devote more time and effort to long-term planning and updating their operations. Hopefully, their future actions will match their intentions.

Until very recently, the manufacturing function was treated as a stepchild of the enterprise, largely neglected in strategic planning. Although close to 75 percent of a typical manufacturing company's assets are directly utilized in the manufacturing process, most companies have not developed a strategy to utilize these assets to optimum advantage. With rapidly advancing manufacturing technology and encroaching competition from abroad, manufacturing planning must become a key component of a company's planning program.

Solid strategic planning can be very cost-effective. It is essential for a successful updating program and can help avoid making expensive mistakes. To the surprise of many executives, such a program can improve the effectiveness and profitability of a manufacturing enterprise even if it is decided *not* to acquire any new, automated equipment.

When considering the initiation of an updating program, effective strategic planning becomes even more vitally important than is normally the case. The reasons include the following:

- The significant and intrusive impact of automation on all functions of a manufacturing enterprise, not just the shop floor
- The high ultimate cost of a comprehensive automation program
- The long lead time required to fully implement an automation program
- The high cost of correcting mistakes resulting from inadequate planning
- The radical overhaul of all processes of the operation
- The drastic changes in relationships within and among the various layers of an organization
- The many obstacles that threaten to lead to failure—unless fully anticipated and properly dealt with in a detailed plan

Proper planning must take into account numerous factors affecting the manufacturing enterprise. These include new demand patterns, new competition, different product mix, different economies of scale, shorter product life cycles, greater customization of products, and demands for higher quality.

Embarking on a factory updating program is not a tactical decision, nor is it mainly a technical one. It usually will require a complete functional and organizational overhaul of the whole company, as well as a reexamination of a company's objectives and the means and methods for pursuing those objectives. It will involve a major, long-term commitment that will have a significant impact on the future of the company.

The Updating Planning Process

An updating program can be viewed as a unique, special-purpose strategic plan combined with an implementation plan that is aimed at upgrading the company into a more viable and profitable manufacturing enterprise.

Preparing an updating program is not a task that can simply be delegated to a group of professional planners as a staff assignment. It should be initiated by the Chief Executive Officer (CEO) or another top executive and should involve all layers of the organization. Although the process starts at the top, subsequent planning and implementation should proceed mostly from the bottom up.

To be successful, there must be highly visible total commitment on the part of top management. Such commitment should include active participation by the CEO and other general managers in the planning effort on a continuing basis throughout the planning period—not just initial financial approval and the appointment of a planning team. General management should provide direction and guidance to the planning team, be accessible for consultation, communicate interim progress results to all employees, and emphasize the importance they place on the updating program for the future of the company.

The planning process should cover the five steps outlined below.

Step 1

A thorough situation analysis and a critical evaluation—indicating strengths and weaknesses—of the following elements of the enterprise are required:

- Resources at the company's disposal, such as the following:
  - Financial resources
  - Plants and equipment
  - Warehouses and offices
  - Patents and trademarks
  - Proprietary technology
  - In-house developed or adapted equipment

- □ Technical expertise, i.e., product design, engineering, and Research and Development (R & D)
- □ Management talent and employee skills and morale
- □ Reputation and customer loyalty
- Manufacturing processes, materials handling, purchasing, accounting, scheduling, marketing, sales, order processing and all other functions directly or indirectly related to the manufacturing operation
- Product line, product life cycles, and product features and quality
- Past, present, and anticipated markets for the company's products, and, in view of the accelerating globalization of business, potential markets abroad
- Competitive standing of the company generally and of each of its products relative to imported products as well as domestically made products
- Relationships between management and labor, as well as interrelationships within these two groups

As part of this first step, the company will often have to perform an operational audit, complete a market research survey, and conduct a technology study. The operational audit should include an evaluation of such performance indicators as efficiency, profitability, flexibility, and innovativeness of all aspects of the enterprise. The market survey should be concerned with the outlook for changes in products, markets, and competition. The technology study should deal with new manufacturing techniques, processes, and equipment.

All of this will require the combined efforts of a large number of people in the organization. It also may require outside assistance from consultants with specialized expertise in strategic planning, operational audits, market research, public image audits, and/or manufacturing technology.

In fact, in many cases it will be preferable to hire an outside consultant, especially to perform the operational audit. An objective consultant with a high degree of professional integrity is more likely to arrive at an unbiased evaluation than in-house staff executives who may feel constrained from pointing out serious deficiencies in their own organization.

Step 2

The next step is a decision-making process by top management that could result in "reinventing" the enterprise. It consists of determining—utilizing the results of Step 1—the company's basic mission and management philosophy, and specific guidelines for the company's future operations. The following questions should be asked:

- Should the company continue in its present type of business?
- What general objectives and specific goals should the company pursue?
- How should the company position itself competitively in the marketplace as regards customer service and the price, quality, and variety of the products to be offered?
- Which types of customers should the company concentrate on and in which approximate priorities?
- Which types of products should be manufactured over the next 5 to 10 years and in roughly what proportion?
- Which types of technology, expertise, and skills will be needed?
- Which types of capital equipment will be required in the factory and in other functions?
- Which type of manufacturing and distribution facilities will be needed, and how many, what size, and in which locations?
- What type of worker, how many workers, and what financial resources will be needed?

It should be noted that the seventh item on the preceding list—capital equipment—is the first time that a preliminary decision is required that is concerned with the degree of sophistication of the equipment used in the manufacturing process. In fact, it has been said that many of the benefits of the updating process are usually derived from organizational changes, while technical improvements contribute a much smaller portion.

There will have to be a considerable amount of iteration among the items listed for Step 2 to make sure that they all fit harmoniously and ultimately will result in a consistent, integrated plan for updating the enterprise. It is important to make sure the guidelines reflect, as much as possible, anticipated rather than current market conditions. In addition, if it is feasible, the planned manufacturing operation should incorporate ample flexibility in production capabilities so as to be able to accommodate changes in market requirements.

Another reason for incorporating adequate flexibility in the planned installation process is to allow for the impact of continuing rapid changes in technology. Since the planning process could take as long as several years, depending on the complexity and comprehensiveness of the updating effort, new technology may emerge in the interim that will require changes in equipment to be specified as well as new interfaces to integrate this new equipment.

Step 3

The third step in preparing the plan is to compare the results of Steps 1 and 2, and determine:

- Which elements (company assets) needed to implement the plan are already in place and can be used with only minor modifications?
- Which elements will require major changes before they can be used?
- Which elements are not useful and should be sold or scrapped?
- Which completely new elements must be acquired?

This third step should include a cost-benefit analysis, discussed in Chap. 11, as well as the preparation of a financial plan to outline how the updating program will be financed.

Step 4

The fourth step consists of preparing a plan detailing how and when the decisions arrived at in Step 3 are going to be implemented. Most of this plan will constitute the manufacturing plan and will specify the extent to which automation is warranted.

As indicated previously, advanced technology should be "pulled," i.e., based on need, rather than "pushed," i.e., based on availability. Automation should always be preceded by an attempt to simplify and improve all operations, and to redesign products and processes to facilitate automation.

The importance of a major effort to first simplify all operations before considering the introduction of automated equipment cannot be stressed too strongly. Major improvements in operational effectiveness and bottom-line profitability have been achieved by many companies before—and even without—installing any new automated equipment. Automation should be introduced selectively, only where it is cost-effective and clearly improves flexibility, speed, and/or quality.

Effective utilization of the new automation technology requires the complete integration of all company functions and processes—not just manufacturing—into a smoothly operating, highly efficient system dedicated to achieve the stated company objectives.

A number of manufacturing firms have failed in their efforts to update their operation because they tried to install new technology, i.e., automated equipment, without making the necessary changes in the way their organization functions. Such simplistic attempts are often counterproductive and have been responsible for setbacks in the updating process in the U.S. manufacturing sector.

Unless the enterprise is rather large and has an in-house staff that is fully acquainted with automated equipment and with all aspects of the automation planning and implementation process, the preparation of the manufacturing plan is likely to require outside assistance. Such assistance is covered in Chap. 13.

Step 5

The final step in the planning process involves preparing a program for systematically monitoring progress in implementing the plan and revising and updating it on a regular basis. Such monitoring can be facilitated by incorporating in the updating program a set of mileposts that specify a number of timed identifiable and quantifiable objectives. As a practical mater, it is advisable to also prepare a contingency plan that will help anticipate breakdowns in the newly automated process and offer solutions for a variety of potential problems.

It is important to try to minimize the disruption of current operations during the implementation of an updating program. This means that the conversion process should be carefully scheduled for each function and each activity.

Ideally, the planning process for updating a manufacturing enterprise should be comprehensive, i.e., it should cover the entire operation, not just a small part of it. Such comprehensive planning tends to be more cost-effective and will help avoid problems later on in updating other parts of the enterprise and in integrating the various separate parts into a smoothly functioning manufacturing operation.

However, comprehensive planning does not necessarily have to be followed up with comprehensive implementation. In fact, time-phased implementation of the master plan over a period of several years may not only be mandated by limited financial resources, but it also has several advantages. It is less disruptive of current operations; it provides a beneficial transition period for management and workers to gradually adjust to the new system; and it facilitates the process of making adjustments and solving the numerous problems that are bound to occur during the run-in period.

As long as the updating plan has been thought out properly and provision has been made for future link-ups and interfaces between the various parts of the total planned system, such a phased implementation process should work smoothly. It is likely to result initially in so-called islands of automation that can later be linked up into a more completely integrated operation.

In some cases it may not be feasible to prepare a comprehensive plan, and top management may decide to initiate a partial updating program. This will necessitate that management choose which part of the enterprise to concentrate its effort on.

Generally speaking, it is best to first automate processes which are likely to benefit most from such a partial updating program. Efforts can be directed toward a particular type of manufacturing process or a particular product group. Careful attention should be paid to blending automated equipment and new methodology with nonautomated equipment and current procedures, and to outlining the role of human workers in such a mixed-type operation.

Simulation

Computer-aided simulation is a unique tool that can be extremely helpful and cost-effective in preparing an updating plan. In fact, computer-aided simulation is the only feasible method for analyzing a proposed complex automated installation in a timely manner that is understandable to executives who are not trained in simulation methodology.

Simulation affords a computer-generated dynamic pictorial view on a computer screen of a proposed system and provides insight into how this system works. It can answer "what if" questions concerning almost any aspect of the system being modeled, including system throughput, equipment-utilization rates, bottlenecks, and the effect of random occurrences.

Although originally introduced more than two decades ago, simulation was little used in manufacturing until recently because it was cumbersome to apply and required computer-programming skills. However, during the past several years special user-friendly simulation software has been developed and simulation is now rapidly becoming a popular, powerful, essential tool.

Simulation can be used not only to plan a manufacturing layout and select equipment, but also as an aid in balancing the various components of an existing installation, troubleshooting the process, and modifying and expanding the whole manufacturing operation.

Further advances in simulation technology promise to make this tool even more useful. Recently developed three-dimensional (3-D) animation and graphics simulation programs are a big improvement over two-dimensional (2-D) programs. Although 3-D programs are still less user-friendly than 2-D programs, it is anticipated that it will soon become easier to program 3-D models. Work is also under way to add time as a fourth dimension so that it will be possible to simulate time-based activities such as scheduling.

There are a number of off-the-shelf simulation software packages available that greatly simplify the task of conducting a simulation program. However, if in-house staff expertise is limited and/or system-throughput requirements are not expected to change frequently, it may be worthwhile to hire a consulting firm that specializes in simulation.

The Planning Team

Most manufacturing companies that have embarked on updating their operation have found that an "automation champion" or "initial agent for change" is essential for success. Ideally he or she should:

- Be a relatively high-ranking executive—or at least a middle-level manager with strong backing from a vice president
- Be a vice president, department head, or staff engineer
- Be a long-term employee with intimate knowledge of the organization and its inner workings
- Have good, general knowledge of the manufacturing process and advanced technology
- Be good at sales and skilled at making effective presentations to top management
- Be well liked and respected throughout the organization
- Be an effective coordinator who is interdepartmentally oriented
- Have strong management and human resources skills
- Be decisive, energetic, enthusiastic, and capable of inspiring others into concerted action
- Have a creative mind and positive, can-do attitude
- Be a resourceful problem solver who enjoys a challenge

- Be willing to take considerable risk
- Be a strong leader who is able and willing to "take ownership" of an automation project
- Be totally convinced of the practical value of automation technology

Since no single person is likely to be available who combines all of these qualifications, a compromise will have to be made in selecting the team leader and some of the gaps will have to be filled by others in supporting roles.

In some companies that are ripe for automation, a suitable team leader may develop spontaneously—a fortuitous event that should be properly and quickly exploited by top management by formally appointing that person to take charge of the updating process. In other companies the start of this process may have to be postponed until a team leader can be groomed.

It is important that the team leader report directly to top general management, usually the CEO or Chief Operating Officer (COO), and be given full authority and the support needed to fulfill his or her mission. In addition to strong support and commitment from the CEO and COO, the team leader may also need a "sponsor," a top executive who has the authority and resources to initiate the project, protect it when opposition develops, and guide it when serious problems must be overcome.

The team leader must be provided with adequate technical, administrative, and financial support, and must be given authority to act across departmental boundaries. His or her first task is to assemble a multidisciplinary planning and implementation task force consisting of individuals with specific expertise needed for the project.

The primary assistant of the team leader is preferably a technical and information expert, i.e., a systems engineer who is thoroughly familiar with manufacturing automation technology and computerized systems, and who can act as the team's guru and coordinator. Other specialists often included as team members are an industrial engineer, automation engineer, manufacturing engineer, software expert, quality control engineer, financial analyst, and human resources specialist.

At an early stage the team should establish close contact with the production department which will ultimately be responsible for running the updated manufacturing operation. As a result, its personnel will begin to identify with the emerging new facility and give the program their full support.

Planning a comprehensive updating program is a formidable task that can take 1 or more years, and requires an intensive effort. This means that most members of the planning team must be involved in their task on a full-time basis. However, a relatively simple program that is limited to a small portion of the manufacturing process would require much less time and effort, and might be managed by a team of mostly part-timers.

The team will be responsible for defining the scope of the project and preparing the conceptual and detailed designs of the updated facility. They will define and prioritize the various component subprojects and coordinate all efforts in the organization that are required for the project. Periodically the team will make formal presentations to top management to gain approval for the program they develop, report progress, present options, and solicit continued support.

An excellent way for the team to get started with its mission is to review the "triggers" that in many cases lead top management initially to consider the possible need for updating the enterprise. Typical triggers include:

- A serious technical problem such as a product recall
- A significant loss of market share to a competitor
- A sudden increase in the cost of a manufacturing input, such as happened at the time of the energy crisis
- A shortage of manufacturing capacity
- The introduction of a new product or product line

Responsibility for overall guidance for the updating project should be lodged in a steering committee or similar offshoot from the company's strategic planning group. It should have representation from each manufacturing division and from several relevant functional groups, including engineering, data processing, quality assurance, finance, etc.

This committee should establish goals, monitor progress, and help coordinate the involvement of the various plants, divisions, and departments in the updating planning and implementation process. Special attention should be devoted to the relationship between the updating project and the company's regular strategic planning process. Depending on the anticipated scope of the project, the team leader may have to participate in the preparation of the strategic plan since his or her project is likely to constitute a major or even dominant component of that plan.

It should be noted that the usefulness of the planning team may extend beyond the start-up of the updated operation. Problems are bound to crop up during the first several months of production—depending on the complexity of the new process—that can best be handled by the people who planned and designed the system. Also, it is usually advisable to limit production initially to a single shift so that any needed adjustments can be made during the off-hours.

Since each company and its needs are unique, the foregoing must be considered as only a rough outline of the updating planning process. Adjustments will have to be made to reflect the wide variety of circumstances, both internal and external, of each individual manufacturing enterprise.

Each company will have to take the necessary time and launch a major effort to develop its own tailor-made updating program. Unfortunately, off-the-shelf packages to update a company or automate its operations do not exist.

Factors that will influence the chances of success of an updating program—as well as the time it will take to implement it—include the degree of motivation and participation of top management; the extent of their personal knowledge of new manufacturing technology and computers; their attitude toward innovation, risk taking, and a more collaborative style of management; their willingness to take a long-range view of profitability; and their ability to do visionary thinking.

9
The Updated Manufacturing Plant

Since progress in updating the manufacturing sector is still in its infancy and innovations continue to be made at a rapid pace, it is difficult to predict with any degree of certainty how the new technologies and methodologies will affect the manufacturing plant buildings that are going to be constructed and the processes that will be installed in those plants. The impacts are likely to vary widely by manufacturing subsector and will depend on how comprehensive and far-reaching the changes will be.

Based on what has taken place so far and on analyses of typical updating programs, a set of possible impacts have been formulated. This may give us at least a partial idea of what the manufacturing scene could begin to look like over the years ahead.

Plant Buildings

The introduction of automation is likely to affect the number and size of plants to be constructed, their location and design, and the environmental conditions within these plants.

Construction of New Plants

The percentage of automation equipment that will be installed in existing plants versus in completely new plants is difficult to anticipate. Several prominent manufacturing companies have constructed new,

107

advanced automated plants while several equally prominent companies have made automation showcases out of old plants.

New plants will be designed increasingly from the inside out, i.e., the manufacturing process will determine the specifications of the plant building. At the same time, since the products to be manufactured in the plant will change more rapidly and frequently than in the past, the buildings must be flexible enough to accommodate the resulting changes in the manufacturing process.

Automating an existing plant will not produce quite the same benefits as building a completely new plant but may still be cost-effective; it has been estimated that the former process will achieve about 80 percent of the benefits of the latter. Also, in some cases, an existing plant cannot accommodate the new, automated equipment and a completely new plant will have to be designed.

However, the following factors make it likely that at least a sizable portion of automation equipment will be installed in existing plants, usually on a gradual basis:

- New plants are very costly.

- New plants usually require a complete reorganization of the company or a division and, thus, may not be considered feasible.

- Old equipment in an existing plant usually is gradually replaced section by section with new equipment—in case it is decided to introduce automation on a piecemeal basis.

Plant Space and Size

The spread of factory automation is expected to result in a decentralization of the production process: Manufacturing is likely to take place generally in a much larger number of smaller, widely dispersed processing units. This decentralization will occur because economies of scale will lose some of their relevance: The automated factory makes it possible to economically produce items in smaller batches and, ultimately, to custom-design products to individual requirements.

The dispersal of manufacturing—together with the dispersal of office work, aided by rapid advances in communications—may slow the urbanization process and result in the spreading out of the population away from large cities.

The expected shift from mass production to batch and even customized production will result in reducing the average size of most manufacturing plants. However, some of the automated plants will still be quite large.

The introduction of the Just-in-Time (JIT) system and the installation of automated manufacturing and warehousing equipment is expected to reduce the need for space significantly—perhaps by 20 percent over the next decade. This, in turn, may tend to reduce the demand for new plants and warehouses as well as expansion of existing facilities.

Plant Location

Factors that will have an impact on the preferred location of automated plants are changes in the types of employees who will work in the automated plants, a strengthening of the bonds between manufacturing plants and suppliers, a reduction in average plant size, changes in the appearance of plants, and an increased emphasis on customer service. The following are some of the expected trends:

- Closer proximity to technically skilled workers and professional and managerial personnel, rather than low-wage and blue-collar labor.
- Closer proximity to urban markets. Plants will be more often located in areas with a relatively high quality of life so that the companies will be better able to attract the necessary personnel.
- Closer proximity to suppliers of parts, components, and raw materials. This change will take place because of the adoption of JIT inventory systems, the need for higher quality and more uniform products, and more frequent changes in product design.
- Proliferation of microfactories in certain industries. Highly automated, small factories with a narrow, specialized product focus will be built near major markets.

Plant Design and Siting

Manufacturers will need to upgrade the quality and accommodations of their plants because of the larger number of more skilled and better educated employees. The plant will often more closely resemble a Research and Development (R & D) laboratory than a present-day typical factory building. Changes will include better lighted and more cheerful employee-receiving and -socializing areas, greater use of colors and signs, better building security, and fewer entrances.

The expected lowering of the barrier between white- and blue-collar workers will be reflected in the design of the building. Both types of

employees will enter through the same doors and eat in the same
cafeteria. In addition, the environment in which they work will be more
similar.

The building's exterior will also be more pleasing aesthetically and
the building will be better sited. This includes landscaping and other
features to make it more attractive to the scientists and engineers who
will work there, as well as—in some cases—to the surrounding urban
neighborhood.

Although the new type of factories will probably be smaller, the factories will be more expensive per square foot since they will be more sophisticated technically and more amenities will be offered to their
occupants. The factories will be integrated with the R & D space and
offices, and will sometimes have the capability of being easily converted
from one use to another.

Environmental Conditions in the Plant

In some factories, the virtual absence of human production workers in
certain sections of the automated plant may reduce the need for lighting, heating, air conditioning, etc. However, it is expected that usually
there will be a *greater* need for the following improved environmental
conditions:

- The plants will require a reduction in vibration, e.g., heavy material-
handling equipment may have to be floor mounted instead of sus-
pended from overhead beams, because of the closer tolerances
needed by automated equipment.

- The plants will have positive air pressure and may require dust collection and other special equipment to reduce air contamination, e.g.,
particulates and corrosive gases.

- Heating, Ventilating, and Air Conditioning (HVAC) systems will be
more sophisticated to provide better humidity and temperature controls. These are needed to ensure trouble-free functioning of automated equipment, higher product quality, and a better environment
for the technical personnel.

- The plants will have better noise control and task lighting in view of
the greater use of computers and terminals throughout the facilities.

- The plants will have better shielding of electrical and electromagnetic
noise from lighting fixtures, transformers, motors, welding equip-

ment, etc., that may interfere with the proper functioning of robots, computers, and other automation equipment.

- Special attention will be given to safety standards to protect employees in their interaction with the automated equipment.

In industries where internal environmental factors such as temperature, humidity, and airborne particles are of critical importance to the production process, the controls of such factors must be closely integrated with the controls of the production process. This applies not only to clean room operations, but also to food, beverage, electronics, fine chemicals, and pharmaceuticals-processing plants.

Another area that needs special attention is the supply of electrical power. In data processing centers, computer equipment is normally protected from power surges, voltage fluctuations, line transients, and similar pollutants by an Uninterruptible Power System (UPS). As computers spread out onto the plant floor, it becomes necessary to install a computer-grade local area UPS that provides "clean" power throughout the entire Local Area Network (LAN) system. Unless the equipment is properly protected, such power pollutants would result in lost data, equipment downtime, increased service costs, and shortened computer life.

Also, with the continuing miniaturization of semiconductor components and their increasing density, automation controls are becoming more vulnerable to the background of electrical disturbances that is created by factory machinery. Reducing this noise pass-through will require the installation of power conditioners.

The Manufacturing Process

Flexible manufacturing equipment makes it possible to almost instantaneously change the specifications of each part or product being manufactured. As a result, such automated plants are extremely versatile and are able to achieve almost the same advantages, such as high speed and low cost, as "hard" mass-production plants while producing a great variety of products of superior quality in very small batches of identical products. Eventually it should be possible to produce a single, "customized" item at almost the same cost as a mass-produced item.

One of the reasons why the automated factory will greatly increase manufacturing efficiency is its ability to move items to be processed much more rapidly through the various production stages and to increase the equipment utilization rate. At present, a part in a metal-working shop is typically being worked on less than 5 percent of the time. In addition, most capital equipment in metal-working facilities is being utilized only 6 percent of the time, because of its specialized, nonflexible nature, and because no second or third shifts are being run, and equipment is idle even during the first shift due to employee vacations, holidays, etc.

The anticipated increase in manufacturing flexibility and efficiency comes at a time when consumers are beginning to demand a much greater degree of product diversification and customization. It can be expected, therefore, that product-design innovations will be more frequent, product life cycles will be shortened, a larger number of new products will be introduced, and a greater variety of models, sizes, and colors will become available. This also means that it will be easier for small entrepreneurs to quickly move into and out of new products as dictated by changes in demand and, thus, that competition will increase. In addition, the quality of parts, components, and finished products will be higher, resulting in fewer returns, less of a need for repairs and replacement parts, and less waste and scrappage.

It is interesting to note that, whereas the output of manufacturing will become *more diversified,* the equipment used in the manufacturing process will become *more standardized.* Product diversification will be accomplished by the software that controls the standardized, versatile equipment.

In view of the above, it is readily apparent that factory automation will have a profound impact on the scale of the manufacturing process. Manufacturing can be divided into four types according to the number of items being processed at any one time:

- *Job shop or customized production.* Only one or a few items are made at any one time; the estimated process efficiency is 8 percent.[1]

- *Batch production.* Small to intermediate quantities of the same product are made; the estimated process efficiency is 6 percent. This process accounts for 75 percent of the value of all manufacturing output of discrete engineering products.

- *Mass production.* Large quantities of discrete items are made; the estimated process efficiency is 22 percent.

- *Continuous flow.* This process is characterized by an endless flow of a bulk product without any interruptions, such as in an oil refinery and

[1]Process efficiency refers to the percentage of time a piece of equipment is actually used in the production process.

certain chemical plants; the estimated process efficiency is up to 96 percent.

It is expected that the number of mass-production plants and—to a lesser extent—job shops in existence now will gradually decline, although both of these production methods will probably never be completely eliminated. Their place will be taken by versatile, mostly smaller scale, fully automated plants that are more akin, but vastly superior, to a batch-production operation. Many of these plants will eventually operate around-the-clock to produce a continuous outpouring of a frequently changing product mix. Their typical output will be in lot sizes ranging between 100 and 10,000 units per year.

Products will be customized to reflect not only rapid changes in consumer preferences but also the specific requirements of different end-use applications, e.g., components can be tailor-made to best fit any one of a variety of products into which they will be integrated.

As regards the role of robots in the four types of production processes, the more sophisticated robots will be used mostly in the new, automated batch-type production facilities, especially for assembly, machine loading and unloading, and other types of material handling. Less sophisticated robots will be used in mass production plants for pick and place, loading and unloading machine tools, and very simple assembly. For the time being, robots will not be sophisticated enough to be used for most job-shop applications that require highly skilled and specialized human operators. Few robots will be needed in continuous-flow process plants.

10
Human Resources

With the current emphasis on advanced manufacturing technology, it is easy to lose sight of the fact that the human worker is still the key to the successful updating of a manufacturing enterprise. Automation failures can usually be traced to failures in the human resources area, rather than in technology. The changes that will be required in all aspects of human resources (H.R.) are far more crucial—and are far more difficult to accomplish—than the technical changes that are to be made in the manufacturing process.

Japanese manufacturing companies have proven the effectiveness of some of their policies and practices in the H.R. area. It has been estimated that technology accounts for only 15 to 20 percent of Japan's productivity lead in certain sectors over the United States; better management accounts for the rest.

U.S. manufacturing can no longer afford to handicap itself with internal strife and inadequate communication between management and labor, engineering and manufacturing, sales and manufacturing, and between other elements of an enterprise. In order to achieve the results expected from automation, a comprehensive, systematic program must be undertaken to completely revamp the way a manufacturing enterprise is managed and to cultivate a new type of employee.

Implementing an updating program will result in a large number of changes in the manner in which a manufacturing enterprise operates. Some of the likely changes that will directly or indirectly affect the human resources area in varying degrees are reviewed in this chapter.

115

A New Type of Employee

One of the most significant impacts of automation will be on the number and types of employees needed to run the new plants. Although fears of mass unemployment are definitely not warranted at this time, the total number of people engaged in the manufacturing sector most likely will drop, just as the number of agricultural workers dropped as a result of farm mechanization.

However, the decline will be gradual—at least initially—and will be offset to a substantial extent by an increase in demand for employees in other economic sectors that interact with manufacturing. In addition, there is no reason why any excess labor cannot be absorbed by increasing the economy's total output of goods and services, and/or by reducing the length of the workweek.

A much more potentially damaging effect of automation will be the expected steep decline in the demand for unskilled and semiskilled blue-collar workers. This problem will have to be dealt with by means of attrition, retraining, and financial support programs.

The work performed by a typical factory employee will be less routine, repetitive, and physical in nature. His or her tasks will include monitoring, troubleshooting, and maintaining a variety of highly automated equipment. He or she will be involved with the Computer-Aided Manufacturing (CAM) process, Manufacturing Resources Planning (MRP-II), and other sophisticated processes utilized in an updated manufacturing operation.

As a result, the qualifications of these employees will be quite different from those of today's blue-collar workers. Job requirements will include:

- Substantial basic technical education and knowledge
- Specific knowledge of the automated equipment they have to deal with, including computers
- Willingness to learn new technology and new skills on a continuing basis
- Ability to troubleshoot equipment
- Ability to anticipate potential equipment malfunctioning and take preventive measures
- Ability to perform their tasks without close supervision and direction, including making decisions
- Ability to function as a cooperative member of a team
- Flexibility and willingness to perform a variety of tasks as needed

- A highly positive attitude to their work and to the organization they work for

The last item is the most important of the job requirements.

The role of midlevel managers will also change. Many such positions will be eliminated. Some of the remaining managers will become operations specialists, e.g., capable of managing data bases, and will act more as consultants than as traditional supervisors.

There will be a steep rise in the demand for engineers and other highly trained people. They will be needed to plan the various processing and assembly operations and to program the automated equipment.

With the increasing complexity of the manufacturing process, a new type of "automated factory" engineer will be required. This engineer's expertise will resemble that of a traditional industrial engineer, but the new type of engineer will have additional training in computers and electronic information and control systems, as well as in robots and other automation equipment. At least some of them will also need training in management and H.R. skills.

Such multidisciplinary manufacturing engineers will be responsible for the proper functioning of automated plants and will also have to interact with a variety of other functional areas of the organization. Since it will be extremely important to minimize plant shutdowns, these engineers will pay special attention to ensuring a high degree of reliability and up-time of the costly, complex equipment of the typical sophisticated manufacturing installation. In addition, they will be heavily involved in equipment monitoring and preventive maintenance.

These engineers will participate actively in planning and designing the automated production process, and overseeing its installation. They will play an especially important role in determining which—and to what extent—manufacturing functions and processes are suitable for automation, and in ensuring the harmonious integration of all components so as to achieve optimum productivity and product quality at the lowest cost.

Changes Affecting Human Resources

The evolving updated manufacturing enterprise will undergo a large number of changes that will affect the human resources area. Some of these changes are:

- There will be substantially more investment in capital equipment per employee.

- Uninterrupted functioning of the manufacturing operation will have greater importance.

- The malfunction of any part of the production system will have more costly consequences for the whole enterprise.

- There will be higher efficiency, with less scrap, fewer rejects, etc.

- The final product will be of higher quality.

- All the functions and activities will be interdependent and integrated.

- There will be more and better interaction and cooperation between management and the work force, among employees, and among the various functions and departments of the enterprise.

- Many tasks formerly performed by humans on the factory floor as well as in all other areas will be taken over by autonomous, computer-controlled machines.

- More decisions will be made by computers with Artificial Intelligence (AI) and Expert Systems (ESs) capability, with humans retaining responsibility only for override and program-change decisions.

- The organization will become less hierarchical, and the style of management will become more participatory.

- There will be fewer layers of management and a fading of the distinction between managers/professionals and workers.

- There will be a blurring of line and staff responsibilities, e.g., a staff engineer will design and program the manufacturing of products from his or her graphics workstation (a line function), while a manufacturing line manager will monitor the manufacturing process for problems (more a staff function).

- Technical and operating information stored in data bases will be widely and instantaneously available to employees at all levels in a form most useful for their particular needs.

- Managers will lose some of their authority and power, while workers at lower levels will act more like managers, have greater authority and responsibility, and make more operations decisions.

- There will be fewer job classifications and broader job scopes.

- Many employees will have to perform multiple tasks, requiring multiple skills.

- More work will be performed in team format; teams will be self-managed and responsible for the entire product, not just some of its parts and components.

- Pay differentials will be based more on the number of skills an employee has than on the individual's job classification within a skill.

As is apparent from the above list, automation—and updating in general—will change in a major way how everyone in the enterprise—not just factory workers—will perform their job. The effects of all these changes on the people involved are going to be significant.

If the changes are introduced and implemented skillfully and if the necessary adjustments are made in the H.R. area, the impact on the workforce should be mostly positive. These impacts include:

- The new jobs should be more challenging, less boring, and less tiring physically.

- There should be less mental stress and frustration.

- Employees at lower levels should gain more authority and responsibility.

- Job security and job satisfaction should increase, new opportunities for promotion and transfer should open up, and turnover should decrease.

- Overall, the enterprise should become more productive and competitive.

However, there is considerable scope for just the opposite effect, and, in fact, that is what has happened in many enterprises that have tried to update their operation without proper planning in the H.R. area. One common error is the too rapid introduction of automation without careful preparation of the labor force, resulting in stress, resistance, and even sabotage of the program.

A Subplan for Human Resources

To avoid H.R. problems that can cripple or abort the updating plan, the plan must incorporate a well thought out H.R. subplan that deals effectively with organization, motivation, training, and recruiting.

Organization

A new, less formal, less hierarchical and leaner companywide organizational structure will have to be devised. At the same time a cultural revolution must take place in the enterprise that will be characterized by:

- Less authoritarian relationships
- More "coaching" and less "issuing of orders"
- Effective two-way communications
- Decision making at the lowest level possible
- A spirit of collaboration among all members of the organization
- Greater participation in management by employees at all levels

Greater participation in management can include the formation of quality circles and self-managing teams of workers with almost total control over their work, as well as the appointment of workers' representatives to participate in plant-level and companywide decision making.

Key features of the new organization will be an emphasis on consistently high quality and productivity, continuous improvement and innovation, customer satisfaction, and commitment to the success of the enterprise.

Motivation

Most U.S. companies have never tried very hard to foster loyalty to the enterprise in their employees. Although there will be fewer employees in a given organization, the proper motivation and attitude of those who remain will be more vital than ever for the success of the enterprise.

Steps must be taken to promote job satisfaction, to secure loyalty to the company and a commitment to its objectives, to forge a real partnership among its participants at all levels, and to nurture a shared corporate culture. The steps should include the following:

- Respond to the apprehensions of employees concerning their new responsibilities and the future of their careers
- Tailor the job content—to the extent that this is feasible—to the employee and make each job as interesting and challenging as possible
- Provide better job security, e.g., limit layoffs for "core" employees, and subcontract for additional workers as needed
- Provide career-path opportunities and facilitate transfers

- Update compensation policies to reflect the new type of factory worker, e.g., replace hourly wages with salaries and tie salaries more closely to completed training, competence, and performance

In addition, each company should attempt to make it easier for its employees to identify with the organization and develop a personal loyalty by adopting a set of explicit basic principles to guide its operations. Such principles could include:

- Genuine concern for the well-being and job security of its employees
- Adherence to a code of morals and ethics in its business dealings
- Regard for the impact of the company's activities on the environment
- Focus on the long-range success of the company as opposed to short-term profitability

Training

It has been estimated that the occupational half-life[1] of a typical employee in an automated plant will be only 3 to 5 years, compared to 7 to 10 years in a nonautomated plant. People entering the labor force today must plan on acquiring new skills an average of four or five times during their career. In addition to the problem of accelerating skill obsolescence, the updated manufacturing enterprise will require different and higher skills, as well as a multiplicity of skills on the part of most employees.

As a result, the education and training of current employees as well as new employees will have to become a top priority of a manufacturing enterprise. Such education and training, including retraining and cross-training, i.e., training employees for a variety of tasks, will have to be a continuing process—not just a one-shot program for a specific task. This means that each company must be prepared to allocate considerable resources to what amounts to an investment in its core employees.

Recruiting

In addition to having to develop a new type of employee, a company will have to search for candidates who will fit more easily into the new organization and who possess the needed attributes. Special requirements

---

[1]The time in which one-half of an employee's knowledge and skill becomes obsolete.

include problem-solving skills and the ability to take the initiative, tackle a variety of tasks, work under little or no supervision, and participate effectively in team efforts.

The typical factory employee will be more skilled, more technically oriented, better educated, and, therefore, more highly paid; this also will mean a lessening of the influence of labor unions. Competition for this new type of employee will be keen. These individuals will be difficult to find, and special efforts, including those listed above under "Motivation" and "Training," will be required to attract and retain them.

The Role of the Human Resources Department

A logical instrument for the development and execution of an H.R. subplan is the H.R. department. Unfortunately, many H.R. departments tend to concentrate on administering existing corporate policies and procedures, and are not oriented toward the introduction of new programs. It may be helpful, therefore, to first revamp and strengthen the H.R. department and redefine its role in the organization to include actively managing the H.R. aspects of an updating program as outlined in the subplan above.

H.R. professionals can and should play a major vital role in the updating program. They can devise strategies for changing the organization and its culture, change recruiting criteria, develop training programs, pinpoint people-related obstacles, and advise how to overcome these obstacles.

The management of human resources will become an increasingly important factor in determining the success or failure of an enterprise. The advanced technology needed to make U.S. manufacturing more competitive is—or soon will be—readily available to every enterprise. The key differentiating factor will be the quality and effectiveness of their human resources.

11
Cost Justification

One of the first and most formidable stumbling blocks in evaluating the feasibility of automating a manufacturing enterprise is the question of cost justification. It turns out that, in many cases, conventional cost-benefit calculations appear to indicate that automation is *not* cost effective.

It is necessary, therefore, to clarify the cost-justification issue, to reevaluate the basis for our current methods, and, hopefully, develop a methodology that will help to realistically determine when automation is justified, in which parts of the operation, and to what extent.

Automation Benefits

Although automation is often perceived as synonymous with replacing human workers, this is not its main benefit, though it usually *does* result in a reduction in a company's work force. Since direct labor currently accounts for only a very small percentage of total manufacturing costs, even a significant reduction in labor costs would have a minimal effect on total costs.

The benefits that can be expected from automating—or, more generally, updating—a manufacturing enterprise are surprisingly numerous and diverse. Ultimately, they all will help to make a company more competitive and viable in today's economy. Specific benefits—in addition to a reduction in direct and indirect labor costs—can be classified under the following categories:

Processing operations
- Reduced setup time
- Fewer time-consuming setups

- Easier and better control of production parameters, e.g., automatic adjustment in material feed based on sensing of tool-bit wear and tear
- Reduced processing time
- Fewer processing steps

Inventory and space
- Faster throughput from raw materials to final product
- Reduced inventory of materials, parts, components, work in process, and final product
- Less floor space (because of less equipment as well as less inventory)

Product development
- Greater ability of the manufacturing process to accommodate product-design changes
- Reduced time to move from design concept to manufacture
- Reduced engineering design cost

Equipment utilization
- Higher equipment utilization rate
- Higher equipment productivity
- More total production time, i.e., more work shifts and less affected by vacations, holidays, illness, absenteeism, strikes, and adverse working conditions

Quality
- Higher quality of the finished product
- More consistent quality
- Less rework, scrap and waste, and fewer rejects
- Lower inspection costs
- Lower warranty service costs
- Fewer product returns and recalls
- Fewer customers lost due to dissatisfaction with product quality

Manufacturing flexibility
- Ability to quickly reprogram equipment for different tasks and different product specifications
- Ability to manufacture a wider and more diversified range of models and products on a single production system without lengthy shutdowns for overhauling transfer lines
- Ability to manufacture very small quantities of each of a large variety of customized products (with different colors, sizes, features, and/or options), while retaining the advantage of economies of scale

- Ability to respond more quickly to changes in consumer demand and competitive conditions
- Less rapid obsolescence of equipment, as compared to a "hard," dedicated type of manufacturing operation

Employee morale and effectiveness[1]

Miscellaneous benefits

- Reduced lead time from receipt of order to shipment of product
- Higher reliability of the manufacturing process and more predictable volume of output.
- Increased ease of acquiring, utilizing, and retaining expert knowledge
- Fewer environmental and occupational hazards
- Reduced overall operational uncertainty
- Lower material-handling costs
- Less paper handling and less redundant information

The results of all the benefits enumerated above can be summarized as follows:

- Increased plant capacity
- Lower overhead and lower product cost
- Quicker and more appropriate response to changes in market demand
- Enhanced ability to plan a company's strategy by increasing the company's options in manufacturing a variety of targeted products
- Higher customer satisfaction
- Increased sales volume, improved competitiveness, and a better chance of continued viability as a successful manufacturing enterprise

Some of the benefits of updating an enterprise can be traced directly to a specific type of computer program [e.g., Computer-Aided Design (CAD)—reduced engineering design cost], a certain method [e.g., Just-in-Time (JIT)—less inventory], the process of planning the updating program (e.g., fewer processing steps), a new human resources approach to managing the staff, or the use of computers. Other benefits

---

[1]This is a significant category of benefits that has been covered in Chap. 10.

cannot be linked directly to a specific change but are the result of implementing the overall updating program.

A number of manufacturing experts have tried to quantify some of the benefits of automation. Since the circumstances of each manufacturing enterprise are unique and the extent to which automation is adopted varies, the estimates the experts arrived at show a wide range and provide only a rough idea of the potential benefits. A few examples are included in the two tables. The first shows those where a favorable *decrease* is a consequence of automation; the second shows those which reflect a favorable *increase*.

Decreases	Range, percent
Direct and indirect labor costs	25–88
Product cost	25–75
Inventory	Up to 90
Work in process	30–50
Lead time from order to product shipment	40–60
Machine setup time	Up to 75
Manufacturing lead time	Up to 90
Product warranty costs	10–35
Plant and warehouse space	Up to 50
Time spent by materials within the plant	Up to 95

Increases	Range, percent
Machine efficiency	15–90
Equipment running time	30–100
Overall productivity of capital equipment	200–500

Materials handling is a key function in the manufacturing process generally, and especially in an automated operation. Materials handling typically accounts for about 90 percent of total manufacturing time and for more than 50 percent of a product's cost. Since improvements in this area alone can cut manufacturing costs by up to 40 percent, materials handling must play a central role in any updating program.

Automation Costs

The cost of comprehensively updating a manufacturing enterprise is huge. At the same time, the risk of failure to achieve the expected benefits can be high. However, the risk involved in *not* upgrading an enterprise that desperately needs to be updated is likely to be even higher. It follows that a sound project evaluation is imperative whenever there is an indication that updating may be called for.

Although it is difficult to generalize because of the wide variety of types and sizes of manufacturing enterprises, it may be helpful to list some of the cost estimates that have been mentioned:

- The average cost of a plantwide automation installation may run between $10 and $20 million.
- The average cost of a Flexible Manufacturing System (FMS) has been put at $4 million.
- A single machining work station within an FMS may run at $800,000.

It is not surprising, therefore, that investment cost constitutes one of the biggest obstacles to a management decision to update and that this high cost is responsible to a large extent for the slow pace of automation in the United States. Other costs that tend to be higher for an automated operation should also be carefully considered. They include equipment tooling, repair and maintenance, and employee training.

It has been estimated that companies typically spend:

- Less than 10 percent of their automation investment on planning, system design, and human resources development
- 50 percent on hardware and installation
- 40 percent on software acquisition and development

Up-front costs for an automation program for a manufacturing enterprise with about 500 employees have been estimated to average $500,000, exclusive of hardware and software. These costs include creating a control structure, formulating the plan, establishing standards for the technology to be used, and setting data standards.

Traditional Cost Accounting

Traditional cost-accounting methodology was introduced over a century ago. It was appropriate for the conditions prevailing in manufacturing up to the 1950s: standardized products, slowly changing technology, and a relatively high percentage input of direct labor. Cost accounting was geared to measure the effectiveness of mechanization as a means of replacing human workers in high-volume operations.

During the intervening years, manufacturing has changed considerably, and the pace has quickened over the past three decades. Unfortunately, cost accounting has not kept pace with the rapid changes in manufacturing methods and information technology.

As a result, manufacturing companies are still trying to justify the implementation of automation technology developed during the past decade with cost-benefit criteria that are no longer applicable and, in fact, often produce highly misleading findings. Inability to justify the acquisition of automation equipment by using outmoded cost-benefit criteria remains one of the major obstacles to the rapid introduction of new manufacturing technology.

Commonly used justification methods include the following:

- *Payback.* This is the number of years it will take before estimated annual savings will equal net investment. U.S. manufacturing companies typically will not acquire any equipment unless its cost can be recovered in 2 years or less; this compares with up to 5 years typically used abroad. Yet, the payback period for some automation equipment will often not be less than 5 years.

- *Net present value.* This is the present value of the total estimated savings over the life of the proposed investment, i.e., after allowing for an assumed minimum attractive rate of return, less the initial net investment.

- *Annual value.* This is the net present value converted into a series of equal annual values spread over the life of the project. This method is useful when comparing projects with different lives.

- *Future value.* This is the net present value of the proposed investment, adjusted by means of an assumed interest rate.

- *Rate of return.* Using the same equation as that for obtaining the net present value and assuming the net present value to be zero, it is possible to calculate the expected rate of return for the proposed investment.

All of these traditional cost-justification measures can be characterized as being focused on tactical, short-term (1 to 5 years) benefits, on direct labor, materials, and energy costs, on cost savings, and on the specific project under consideration in isolation within a single department.

As most commonly applied, they suffer from the following serious deficiencies in today's manufacturing environment:

- The tracing, measurement, and allocation of many cost elements (based on direct labor) are inaccurate.
- The value of "intangible" benefits is implicitly assumed to be zero.
- The value of many of the other benefits of updating (listed previously) is similarly not accounted for.
- The value of long-term benefits is disregarded.
- The value of time saved is not considered, even though time has become more important than direct labor.
- No allowance is made for the beneficial effects of a proposed project on other parts of the company.
- No allowance is made for the strategic impact of the proposed investment on the company as a whole.
- The manufacturing process is mistakenly assumed to be working as planned, i.e., quality problems are ignored.
- The cost of overproducing parts and components and of performing unnecessary, no-value producing tasks is disregarded.
- Inventories are considered as an asset, rather than an expense-producing liability.
- No allowance is made for the risk of failure, i.e., probability estimates are not included in the calculations.
- Although the real objective of the enterprise, namely, profit maximization, involves revenue creation as well as cost minimization, only the latter factor is taken into consideration. In other words, it is mistakenly assumed that revenues will not be affected, whether or not the proposed project is implemented, i.e., revenue-enhancing and revenue-loss prevention effects are totally overlooked.

To put the basic weakness of traditional cost-justification methods into proper focus, it is useful to consider the relative benefits obtained from updating the enterprise by each of the four major types of change made in the manufacturing operation.

It has been estimated that only one-fifth of the total benefits can be allocated to a decrease in direct labor and a reduction in waste. Organizational changes account for two-fifths, while the introduction of automated equipment and new processing techniques account for the remaining two-fifths of total benefits. This indicates that traditional cost justification, by concentrating mainly on direct labor, tends to account for only a small portion of all the benefits that can be expected from a successful updating program.

New Approaches

Although the proper cost justification of an updating project is complex, difficult, and subject to uncertainties, this does not mean that such projects must or should proceed on faith alone. A badly planned and economically "unjustified" updating project is likely to have a worse effect on a company than not updating at all. At the same time, efforts to justify a project on the basis of conventional cost-accounting methodology will often result in an incorrect no-go decision.

It follows that there is an urgent need to upgrade the present cost-benefit evaluation process and bring it in tune with newly developing manufacturing systems. There appears to be some disagreement among the experts in the field whether traditional cost-justification methods can be sufficiently updated or whether a totally new approach must be found.

According to some experts, there is nothing basically wrong with, e.g., the discounted cash flow method. It simply needs to be applied more effectively to current manufacturing operations. Other experts, while usually not entirely discarding traditional methods, feel that a completely new method is called for. A number of individuals and groups have tried and are trying to resolve the cost-justification problem and to update cost-accounting procedures for use in automation projects.

Under present conditions, it takes a considerable amount of time and effort, as well as a degree of ingenuity and resourcefulness, to successfully justify the acquisition of an automated manufacturing installation. The following are some of the suggestions that have been made that can help in preparing a more realistic and accurate cost-benefit justification for planning and implementing an updating program:

- Eliminate arbitrary allocations of costs on the basis of direct labor and try to trace all costs to each product over its complete life cycle, i.e., development, manufacturing, distribution, and field support. This will help determine the margin between net cash revenues and the investment required to get the product into production.

- Uncover the many useful data that already exist on the shop floor and in accounting systems but that are hidden by departmental budgeting and other accounting conventions.

- Create detailed cost information for all overhead elements that is comparable in coverage to what has been compiled for direct labor.

- Allocate each overhead expense directly to each physical activity associated with it, rather than linking overhead to the product based on volume measures.

- Determine machine costs on the basis of usage, rather than economic life, and accumulate such costs over the machine's technological life, rather than its depreciable life.

- Assign a dollar value to all intangible benefits: An estimated value—no matter how approximate—is likely to be better than not estimating a value at all.

- Identify the effects of intangible benefits and then try to quantify these effects, e.g., a human-resource benefit such as "higher morale" can be translated into lower turnover, less absenteeism, and higher productivity—all of which *are* quantifiable. Other examples include: Better tracking of parts and components is likely to reduce expediting costs, and better materials-handling control and better scheduling may increase equipment utilization rates and thereby reduce the number of machines needed.

- Include any remaining intangible benefits that cannot be quantified at all, neither directly nor indirectly, on an evaluation grid that includes a do-nothing option. Attempt to give each benefit at least a qualitative rating (excellent to poor) or a comparative rating (better to worse) for each investment option under consideration.

- Make a special effort to quantify the benefits derived from improved quality.

- Break out quality costs and try to assign a value to each of the following items:
  - Failure costs: warranty service, credit processing, scrap, rework, etc.
  - Appraisal costs: quality inspection of products and raw materials.
  - Prevention costs: quality engineering and quality control.

- Trace the benefits of improved quality:
  - Lower inventory costs.
  - Higher customer satisfaction, which in turn results ultimately in larger market share, higher revenue, and higher profitability.

- Accept extended payback periods to allow for the longer life of automation equipment (due to its flexibility) and for the long time period during which automation benefits accrue.

- Select a more realistic (lower) cost-of-capital "hurdle" rate than is frequently used in cost-justification formulas; a high rate tends to favor projects with short-term benefits and penalize flexible automation projects that have a long useful life.

- Evaluate projects in terms of companywide return on assets by taking into account short- and long-term revenue-creating benefits as well as cost savings.

- Expand the cost-evaluation process by including strategic considerations—if they are appropriate—such as the need to enter a new market, remain in a certain market or expand market share, even if the required investment is not going to be cost-effective in the immediate future.

- Add risk analysis, i.e., evaluate the probability of success, and sensitivity analysis, to assess the uncertainties of each project, including "making do" with existing equipment. In conjunction with this suggestion, also prepare a set of best, worst, and base case scenarios as another aid to top management in assessing risk.

- If a company is big enough, try out an updating project on a small scale in one of its departments or plants largely "on faith." If the project's actual cost-effectiveness is sufficiently positive—much more easily determined after than before implementation—the company may then decide to plan and implement such projects on a much larger scale.

- Perform a simulation analysis of the proposed changes. A simulation program can be helpful as part of a cost-justification exercise, at least partly because it forces a thorough analysis of the whole manufacturing process, which facilitates making estimates for each cost and each benefit.

- Ensure cooperation from the entire company. To properly uncover and quantify the true benefits of automation, the cost-justification process should be a strategy-oriented cooperative effort on the part of manufacturing, engineering, marketing, quality control, general management, and the finance/accounting department.

A relatively new approach to cost accounting, called Activity-Based Costing (ABC), is being used by a few companies on an experimental basis. ABC promises to help in justifying investments in automation equipment by allocating costs more realistically. ABC measures costs in minute detail at each step of a process—including reworking defective products and eliminating bottlenecks—and takes into account the cost of scrap, delays, and inefficiencies. Each overhead function is tied directly to a specific product or process.

Ideally, each manufacturing company should install a totally new, modern cost-accounting system that provides better cost information and that captures and quantifies as many of the tangible and intangible benefits of an updated manufacturing system as possible. However, this is an expensive and time-consuming effort that would in any case be only partially effective since the required methodology is still being developed.

In the final analysis, the overriding question is: What must a manufacturing company do to remain competitive? If one or more of its major competitors are installing a sophisticated manufacturing system that is likely to give them a significant edge in satisfying their customers, the company most likely will have to follow suit or risk going out of business. Such a simplified reasoning process is likely to be applicable mainly in the case of a rather small company that has an intimate knowledge of its customers and what must be done to keep them.

In conclusion, it is interesting to note that cost-reduction benefits often are overshadowed among the results of an updating program by other, mostly "intangible" benefits. It is not surprising, therefore, that many successful investments in new manufacturing technology and procedures have been based on "a leap of faith," rather than conventional cost-justification methods. Until a new methodology has been developed, the trick is to recognize when such a leap of faith is warranted for strategic reasons, and when it is not.

12
Misconceptions and Obstacles

The process of updating a manufacturing enterprise is fraught with many dangers and faces serious challenges and obstacles. As a result, attempts to introduce innovations frequently lead to false starts and disappointments. This is extremely unfortunate, and it is one of the major reasons why automation has not made more rapid progress over the past 10 to 20 years in the face of the urgent need for quick and decisive action to improve the competitiveness of U.S. manufacturing.

Misconceptions

Several serious misconceptions about automation have induced some top managers not to consider this approach when updating their operations. Other misconceptions have encouraged other top managers to try to update their enterprise in a manner that almost certainly results in failure, an almost total loss of the investment made, and a firm resolution never to get involved in automation again. A sampling of such misconceptions is presented here.

First Myth.   If labor accounts for only a small percentage of total manufacturing costs, automation is not likely to be of any benefit.

Reality.   In many types of manufacturing operations today, labor represents only a relatively minor cost item, and, therefore, any savings on labor cost will often have little or no impact. However, automation frequently can result in a significant reduction in overhead and other costs;

in addition, automation provides other benefits that are even more important since they may make it possible for a doomed enterprise to revitalize itself.

Second Myth.   If a manufacturer has very short production runs or operates almost as a job shop, automation will provide few, if any, benefits.

Reality.   The concept of factory automation today generally implies a certain degree of flexibility in handling a variety of products. This contrasts with the "hard automation" characterized by transfer lines and other types of dedicated equipment employed in mass production that has been in use for decades. In its most advanced form, a flexible automated manufacturing operation can efficiently produce a sizable number of different products on a custom basis, i.e., quantities as small as a single unit with its own unique combination of customer-ordered specifications (color, size, features, etc.).

Third Myth.   If a factory does not experience any major problems and appears to be working rather efficiently, there is no need to consider automation.

Reality.   Consumers today demand products of a large and constantly changing variety. These changing market demands can often be met only by new manufacturing processes and procedures that are made possible by today's new technology. To remain successful and stay in business, each manufacturer must adapt and employ only the most up-to-date technology.

Fourth Myth.   The true cost-benefit of automation cannot be calculated, and, therefore, all automated equipment must be purchased simply on the basis of management's faith in its ultimate effectiveness.

Reality.   Although realistic cost-benefit calculations are difficult to perform and may not be able to fully account for all the benefits of automation, this does not mean that automation cannot be financially justified.

Fifth Myth.   If your competitors are automating their factories, it is time to install some automated equipment in your own factory.

Reality.   It certainly is a good idea to take notice when your competitors are updating their facilities and to seriously investigate the feasibility of following their lead. However, it would not be advisable to blindly imitate their example, and it certainly would not be wise to simply purchase and install the same equipment they did. The key to successful updating is careful planning that takes into account the individual circumstances of each enterprise. In some cases, automation is not needed and could be counterproductive.

Sixth Myth.   If you are going to update, you may as well install the most sophisticated equipment available today and automate every process that can possibly be automated.

Reality.   The degree of sophistication in automation equipment to be installed in a plant should be determined by a careful evaluation of the individual current and future needs of the manufacturing enterprise and its expected cost-benefit, not by what is technically possible and available.

Seventh Myth.   If capital funds are insufficient to update the complete manufacturing operation, and if there is major concern about the unsettling impact of a complete overhaul on the enterprise, the best approach is to start to automate the most likely process and postpone considering the updating of the total enterprise until some time in the future.

Reality.   There is a tendency to quickly automate one or more processes that seem to be most appropriate and will require only a modest investment. However, the creation of such "islands of automation" can be counterproductive in the long run *unless* they are part of a prior comprehensive updating plan for the total enterprise that provides for the eventual hookup and integration of such islands into a modernized, complete manufacturing operation. The general rule is: Always plan comprehensively; then, if necessary, implement gradually.

Eighth Myth.   Automation simply means the replacement of employees with equipment to perform essentially the same tasks as before, to produce the same products, to serve the same customers, to purchase from the same suppliers, and to use the same yardsticks to measure performance.

Reality.   This myth incorporates several serious misconceptions that can be rebutted as follows:

- Replacing human workers might be counterproductive since they are still the most versatile and adaptable manufacturing resource, and they can perform many tasks far better than any piece of automated equipment.

- Replacing human workers is only one of the possible benefits of auto-mation and is not always cost-effective.
- Automating a factory "as is" without prior in-depth strategic planning might easily result in an automated "buggy whip" plant, an interesting but very costly demonstration of automation that will not help the company remain (or become) a viable, successful enterprise.
- Automating an inefficient manufacturing process without also modi-fying the process itself will result in a high-cost automated *inefficient* manufacturing enterprise.
- Automating the factory floor operation without updating all other aspects of the manufacturing enterprise will often be of little or no benefit.

Ninth Myth. If a company has a rather capable in-house engineering staff, and especially if the company has a rather unique manufacturing installation, there is no need to seek the assistance of outside automa-tion experts in planning the updating process.

Reality. Except for a few giant manufacturing firms, comprehensive in-house automation planning talent is still rare. An outside consultant (not connected with an equipment supplier) often can provide a valu-able service, in collaboration with a company's own staff, in properly planning—and possibly later on in implementing—a comprehensive updating effort.

Tenth Myth. Automation ultimately means the transformation of today's factory into a lights-out fully automated operation that is totally controlled by computers and requires practically no human participa-tion.

Reality. Such an "automated factory," although technically possible, is not likely to become widespread in the foreseeable future—if ever—and probably has only limited application from a cost-benefit point of view. What manufacturers should be striving for instead is to use automation as a valuable tool, in combination with other approaches, whenever and wherever it is likely to be of direct benefit in updating their enterprise to the extent economically warranted.

All of the foregoing misconceptions are dangerous to the well-being of U.S. manufacturing. Some of them could induce Chief Executive Officers (CEOs) to stubbornly continue to do "business as usual" and to overlook the possible contributions that automation and related approaches could make toward keeping their enterprise healthy over the years ahead.

Some of the other misconceptions listed above could lead to blindly adopting an over ambitious or ill-conceived simplistic program that might be even more harmful. Automation is not an end in itself. It is a sophisticated, technologically advanced tool that may help restore competitiveness to a manufacturing enterprise and improve its chances of survival.

Obstacles

As discussed in Chap. 11, the difficulty involved in properly justifying the cost of updating a manufacturing enterprise is a major obstacle that continues to slow down the modernization of U.S. industry. However, it is by no means the only one. In fact, there are a large number and a wide variety of such obstacles. They are classified below under three headings: top management, employees and organizational quirks, and automation technology.

Top Management

Many top managers in the United States—more so than in some other countries—suffer from a number of handicaps and attitudes that tend to hinder the adoption of an updating and automation program:

- Lack of awareness concerning the need to put more emphasis on long-term strategic planning and to become more competitive by means of updating their company
- Aversion to risk-taking, especially in areas where they lack personal knowledge
- Preoccupation with finance and marketing, and exclusion of manufacturing executives from the corporate-planning process
- Preoccupation with mergers and acquisitions instead of concentrating on strengthening their own enterprise
- General lack of knowledge of, and interest in, the manufacturing process, advanced manufacturing technologies, and the use of computers

- Lack of interest in systematically fostering innovation in their organization, including developing new products and utilizing new manufacturing technologies and methods
- Reluctance to modify the existing corporate culture to accommodate the changes required for updating the enterprise
- Unwillingness to tolerate an unsettling complete overhaul of the organizational structure, in addition to automating the manufacturing operation
- Resistance to adopting a decentralized and more cooperative management style
- Failure to recognize the benefits of team-type and cross-disciplinary efforts that typically play a prominent role in an updated enterprise, and to encourage and reward the accomplishments resulting from such efforts
- Insistence on applying traditional cost-justification methods for capital investment programs
- Mistaken impression that the failure of even one major component of an integrated manufacturing process is bound to bring the whole plant to a standstill
- Uncertainty whether the implementation of an automation program will really improve the company's competitive position in the marketplace

Employees and Organizational Quirks

As reviewed in Chap. 10, the updating program will have a far-reaching impact on the working conditions of all employees and on their relationships. Some of these changes will tend to create resistance, especially on the part of middle managers and professionals, that is likely to affect the implementation of the program unless effectively counteracted.

Such changes include lessened authority and power of middle managers, resulting from:

- More equal access to information by all employees
- Bypassing of middle managers in the communication of information between top managers and lower level employees
- Transfer of professional expertise to computerized expert systems

- Upgrading of lower level employees to acting manager status
- Greater dependence of middle managers on the technical experts who build and control the new information systems

Also, middle managers may become somewhat concerned that, in the updated organization, errors at the lowest levels will be quickly communicated directly to top management and that they will be held more accountable for what happens in their area of responsibility.

Additional problems centering on the employees of an enterprise and on the way in which its current organization functions may include:

- Resistance to change and fear of uncertainty
- Concern about the possible upset of the political balance among the various functional groups
- Resistance to participating in teamwork
- Traditional competitive spirit among departments, including reluctance to share information
- Fragmentation of the organization and lack of dynamic interaction to achieve common goals
- A communications gap between nontechnical and technical departments
- Bureaucratic conservatism and adherence to narrowly defined job responsibilities
- A cumbersome decision-making process that hinders the evaluation and adoption of automation programs
- Conservative attitude of many manufacturing managers who are inclined "not to rock the boat" by suggesting radical changes that could backfire and endanger their job security
- A lack of encouragement and reward for risk-taking in the manufacturing area, which reinforces this conservative attitude
- Continued concentration by many manufacturing executives on labor savings and cost cutting rather than increasing market share by offering better products and services
- A highly compartmentalized manufacturing division that tends to aim for the optimization of subsystems rather than of the manufacturing operation as a whole
- Lack of adequate education and hands-on experience in the manufacturing process on the part of many manufacturing engineers

Automation Technology

A number of the obstacles with which manufacturing companies have to struggle are inherent in the automation technology itself:

- The high capital cost of implementing an automation program and the enormous amount of time and concerted effort required—even for a partial updating—tend to be overwhelming and discouraging to top management, and may prevent any action from being taken.

- Mistakes in planning and unexpected major changes in the business environment can be extremely costly and could even lead to the demise of the enterprise.

- Earlier computerization programs of various types experienced high failure rates when they were first introduced, and this carried-over knowledge instills some fear that some Computer-Integrated Manufacturing (CIM) programs might not work properly either.

- Automation technology is still developing rapidly, and this poses the risk that a newly installed system might soon become obsolete.

- At present, tailor-made, off-the-shelf comprehensive installations are not available, and this means that each program requires a time-consuming, costly, custom-made approach.

- Since components must usually be obtained from several vendors of equipment and software, at least some of which are likely to be incompatible with each other, special provisions must be made for appropriate interfaces and the integration of all components into a complete, well-functioning system.

- Experts with multidisciplinary education and experience are needed to devise and install a sophisticated automated system. These experts may well be in short supply. Broadening and deepening the expertise of engineers who lack one or more of the requirements tends to be time-consuming since the learning curve in automation is a long one.

It is obvious that the array of obstacles impeding progress in the United States in updating its manufacturing sector is formidable. Also, the U.S. government—unlike those of some other countries—provides few if any incentives that would facilitate and encourage automation in the private sector.

Nevertheless, a number of U.S. pioneering companies have risen to the challenge and have demonstrated the necessary resolve and ingenuity to overcome these problems and handicaps. If nothing else, pure necessity will gradually force a majority of U.S. manufacturing companies to follow the lead of these pioneers.

13
Outside Assistance

One of the basic decisions to be made when starting to plan an updating program is to what extent outside assistance will be relied upon. There are three possible approaches:

- Utilize the planning and implementation services offered by the manufacturers and vendors of automation equipment
- Call upon the services of one of the large variety of firms that offer assistance but do not supply the needed equipment themselves
- Rely mostly on the company's in-house staff, fortified with newly hired appropriate talent

The specific approach or mix of approaches to be taken should be researched and planned as one of the early steps of the updating process.

Equipment Manufacturers and Vendors

Manufacturers that provide hardware equipment and software programs for inclusion in automated installations can be classified under the following major categories:

- Machine tools
- Materials-handling equipment

- Robots
- Computers
- Controls
- Computer-Aided Design and Computer-Aided Manufacturing (CAD/CAM) and related programs

The acquisition of an automated installation usually requires the purchase of equipment from a variety of specialized manufacturers and vendors. There are about 600 manufacturers of machine tools in the United States of which only a few are large; the top 12 account for about 85 percent of the total output. Five of the more than 70 manufacturers of CAD/CAM equipment account for over 70 percent of the market. There are more than 50 manufacturers of robots, including several major companies; the top six account for about 65 percent of the total number of robots produced. In addition, there are a large number of companies that provide a wide variety of software programs.

Originally, the focus of most equipment manufacturers was very narrow, supplying only a few models of one type of equipment and giving little thought to how their products would be integrated with other components into an automated installation. Even today, many manufacturers still specialize in only a few types of automation equipment. For some of them, such equipment is only a sideline, while for others it is their main business.

Most manufacturers and vendors have begun to offer their customers assistance in planning, selecting, installing, and integrating the equipment they supply. However, many are generally unable and/or unwilling to provide the comprehensive service that is usually needed by their customers.

Vendors still tend to view systems integration as mainly a technical effort aimed at integrating equipment that uses different computer technologies. Yet, most manufacturing companies involved in automation feel that problems related to people and the organization are far more likely to impede the automation process than problems concerning technology. As a result, these companies expect systems-integration services to include the integration of all elements of a manufacturing system, including the human element as well as technology.

Several years ago, abandoning the typical narrow focus of vendors, a few large diversified equipment manufacturers—especially machine-tool builders and materials-handling equipment manufacturers—began to offer a truly all-encompassing automation planning and installation service, with some of them even willing to act as prime contractor. In some cases they have established separate divisions to provide this service. These firms will supply not only the equipment they manufacture themselves, but also any needed equipment made by other manufacturers.

Another approach used by equipment vendors attempting to satisfy their customers' need for a comprehensive automation package has been to enter into affiliations with firms that offer equipment and services that complement their own. Hardware manufacturers typically have allied themselves with software vendors, but affiliations between manufacturers making complementary hardware are also common. The objectives of such cooperative agreements are the integration of technologies, interfacing of products, and then marketing of the products as a joint effort.

The following disadvantages should be considered by a potential customer before deciding to use vendors—whether single-service firms, diversified manufacturers offering a comprehensive service, or affiliated firms—as the main source of assistance when planning and installing a major automated system:

- The equipment manufacturer may be limited in the depth and breadth of its planning and engineering expertise.
- The firm may tend to shortchange its customers on the time and effort devoted to planning an automated operation, especially the strategic aspects of the business enterprise.
- The firm is likely to be biased in selecting its own equipment rather than that of another manufacturer.

On the other hand, most equipment manufacturers and vendors also offer a number of advantages that may outweigh their disadvantages, depending on the circumstances of their potential client company. These advantages are:

- Long-term business stability
- Financial resources
- Possibly lower prices
- Intimate knowledge of its own equipment
- Extensive knowledge about plant floor operations and equipment applications
- Access to support services
- Better ability to guarantee results and assume responsibility
- Easier integration of components
- Faster implementation

Other Assistance

As the need for assistance in automating manufacturing operations—beyond that available from most equipment manufacturers—has continued to grow, an increasing number of firms have begun to offer systems integration and consulting services. These firms have both hardware and software engineering capabilities but do not manufacture or sell automation equipment. They generally are not affiliated with any equipment manufacturers. However, as mentioned previously, a few giant manufacturing firms that include certain types of automation equipment in their product line have established a separate division or subsidiary that specializes in systems integration.

Systems integrators often act mostly in a coordinating and/or consulting capacity. They offer a variety of services ranging from strictly advice and minimal actual involvement to a turnkey automation service.

Specific functions they may perform in addition to consulting include acting as systems architect, prime contractor, project manager, construction manager, and subsystem manager. Their responsibilities vary, depending on the type of firm and the function they perform, and could cover engineering, installation, and performance and financial guarantees.

Most manufacturing companies want to retain control over their own automation project and do not contract for turnkey services. They most often retain systems integrators as consultants and as subcontractors for specific components. Typical consulting tasks include assisting in determining long-term objectives, specifying system requirements, providing technical advice, and developing software programs. Each contract between a manufacturing company and a systems integrator is different and is tailored to the needs of the manufacturing company and the capabilities of the systems integrator.

Types of firms that act as systems integrators include:

- Engineering firms
- Management consultants
- The six largest accounting firms
- Major software houses
- Independent systems firms that specialize in automation
- Divisions of major manufacturers that consume a large quantity of the automation equipment they make as part of their total product line

Engineering Firms

Large, diversified engineering firms that focus at least partly on the manufacturing sector are becoming significant participants in providing comprehensive automation services. Their services are gradually being expanded to include the full range of expertise that is required by manufacturing companies interested in a major updating of their operation. Several well-known engineering and construction firms have established joint ventures with high-tech firms to better serve this new market.

This participation by engineering firms is being driven by changes that are taking place in the manufacturing market sector that they have traditionally served. With plants being designed more and more from the inside out—with primary emphasis on the manufacturing process and its sophisticated and costly equipment—and with the shift towards modernizing existing plants rather than building "green field plants," engineering firms must adapt their services to the change in market requirements or expect to lose market share.

Engineering firms with (1) a strong technological, computerized controls and shop floor/processing orientation, (2) the necessary business planning expertise, and (3) a strong commitment to serving the new market of updating manufacturing installations are likely to be most effective as systems integrators and prime automation contractors.

Other Types of Systems-Integrator Firms

Several of the six largest accounting firms have established separate management consulting divisions that specialize in systems integration for factory automation projects. In some cases they have affiliated themselves with equipment manufacturers to improve their credibility and to be able to offer a more comprehensive service.

There are a large number of independent systems firms that specialize in factory automation. Most of these systems integrators are small and tend to have limited in-house talent with hands-on experience.

They typically specialized originally in a few technologies and limited their integration services to the equipment of a few vendors. As potential clients began to require plantwide integration of a great variety of equipment, these systems integrators expanded the scope of their services. However, most of these small systems integrators are not likely to be equipped to take on primary responsibility for handling complex, comprehensive automation projects. They also do not have the financial resources to guarantee system performance. Nevertheless, small independent systems integrators can perform a number of useful services, mainly as consultants, in assisting a capable in-house staff of a client company in planning and implementing an automation project.

A new type of participant in this market, which has not been mentioned yet, is the high-technology market research firm specializing in factory automation. Such firms do not function as systems integrators, but they provide their clients with information designed to assist them in dealing with the diversity of technologies and equipment available. They do not get involved in planning or implementing automation projects, but they can help select a supplier of automation services and equipment.

Utilizing Systems-Integrator Firms

Outside systems-integrator firms, of whatever type, can often be helpful in providing a more balanced and objective perspective. Such firms can work well with a variety of equipment vendors, tend to be knowledgeable about a range of technologies, and are likely to be more flexible and more committed to their clients' interests than vendors. In addition, their participation will tend to reinforce top management's commitment to the project and help produce and maintain the necessary momentum of the program.

However, to be able to provide a worthwhile service, a systems-integrator firm will require considerable time to fully acquaint itself with the details of its client's operation—and this learning process must be paid for by the client. Another disadvantage of relying heavily on a systems integrator—as discussed more fully in the next section—is that the client company may tend to neglect the participation of its own in-house staff in the automation project. This will affect their ability to properly operate the installation once it is completed.

The extent of responsibility of the systems-integrator firm should be clearly defined as soon as possible after the firm has been selected. Its exact role will depend on the strength and availability of the in-house team: A relatively weak in-house staff will require a strong outside integrator firm. To be effective as a significant contributor, the top representative of the integrator firm must be an active, full-member participant of the client's in-house updating team. In all cases, it is important for the integrator firm to become involved in the updating project as early as possible, i.e., during the planning phase, even if its contribution is anticipated to be made mainly during the implementation phase.

In choosing a systems-integrator firm to help in acquiring an automated installation, a manufacturing company should carefully evaluate the candidate firm's qualifications relative to its own needs. Some of the factors that should be considered include:

- Does the integrator firm have sufficient experience in installing the type of automated process being contemplated?
- Does the firm know the industry sector of the client?
- Has the firm been involved in installations of the same size as the one planned?
- Does the firm have an appropriate multidisciplinary background, including hardware and software, shop floor controls, assembly, or purchasing?
- What was the integrator firm's original orientation, e.g., did it start out in computers, software, machine tools, or materials handling?
- Does the firm have the required breadth of vision as well as depth of specific expertise?
- Is the firm truly objective and unbiased, both as regards types of equipment (no links with equipment manufacturers) and systems and approaches to be used (no blind commitment to automation as a universal cure-all and no preoccupation with a single method or component of automation)?
- Is the firm knowledgeable about the business aspects of a manufacturing enterprise, including strategic planning?
- Is the firm's personnel likely to get along well with the manufacturer's management and its in-house technical staff?

If the manufacturer/client requires a comprehensive assistance package, the systems-integrator firm that is selected should be able to provide a full range of services, including, e.g., conception and design, development of controls, procurement of needed equipment, supervision of the installation process, and overall management of the updating project in collaboration with the client's in-house staff.

In-House Staff Involvement

Ideally speaking, the in-house staff of a manufacturing company should be primarily responsible for planning and installing an automated system as well as the rest of an updating program. Japanese manufacturing companies have proven that this is the best way to proceed. In-house engineers of Japanese manufacturing companies frequently take care of most aspects of the project and rely on vendors only for acquiring the equipment and for assistance in problem solving.

However, proceeding in this manner is possible only if the manufacturer has a relatively large staff of manufacturing engineers who are knowledgeable about the company's requirements and the capability and availability of the various types of automation equipment that may be needed. Japanese manufacturing companies consider the manufacturing design function—which is closely linked with new product design—as a vital component of their operation, and they have on the average three times as many manufacturing engineers on their staff as comparable U.S. firms. As a result, many manufacturing companies in Japan are fully capable of taking primary responsibility for planning and implementing a comprehensive updating program.

As regards most U.S. manufacturing companies, the decision of whether to use outside assistance in proceeding with the updating of their operation is probably the easiest step in the process: Except for a few large companies with an in-house staff that is especially knowledgeable about automation, all candidates for updating will have to obtain at least some outside assistance.

In recent years, more and more companies have, in fact, decided to call upon outside assistance. Their decision is dictated by the complexity of the technology involved and the lack of adequate in-house expertise in all of the issues that must be addressed.

Additional factors are the continuing rapid change in automation technology, the relatively long learning curve in mastering the process of introducing automation, and the net cost savings that can result from hiring expert outside assistance. The weight of all these considerations is reinforced by the current tendency of many manufacturing companies to reduce the size of their in-house engineering staff.

Although utilizing the services of an outside firm can often not be avoided, a determined effort should be made by the client manufacturing company to have its in-house staff play a substantial role in the automation process—even if this would require hiring additional engineers. Lack of sufficient involvement of the client's in-house staff in all phases of the automation project is a frequent cause of failure.

It should be realized that the new installation will have to be run and eventually modified by the in-house staff. Also, only the in-house staff fully comprehends all of the intricacies and peculiarities of the functioning of the client's enterprise, and is therefore uniquely qualified to participate in planning the updating program in the required detail.

An outside consultant should not and cannot be expected to act as a substitute for a well-rounded, capable, committed in-house planning and implementation team, headed by the right "automation champion," as discussed in Chap. 8. Outside assistance also should not be expected to significantly reduce the activities of the in-house planning team during the planning process. Outside assistance only can facilitate and accelerate the process and increase its chances of success. It can do so by supplying missing or inadequate talents and information, by providing balance and an unbiased overview, and by drawing on the lessons learned while assisting previous clients.

It can be categorically stated that it is not possible to either purchase an automated installation from a vendor or hire a systems integrator to completely plan and install an automated plant *without* major involvement on the part of the in-house staff at all levels. The extent of outside assistance that is needed will depend on the strength of the in-house staff and/or the willingness of the management of the manufacturing company to hire additional permanent employees with the required background.

In some instances it may be possible to limit outside assistance to using the services of one or more equipment manufacturers or vendors, as long as the services that are offered are sufficiently comprehensive and of high quality, *and* the manufacturing company's own staff is exceptionally capable and knowledgeable. Advantages of performing the systems-integration functions with in-house staff include better control and coordination, more effective communication, and lower out-of-pocket cost.

In many cases, however, it will be necessary to utilize the services of one of the types of consulting firms covered in the preceding section as well as to deal with the manufacturers and vendors that supply the needed equipment.

Planning and installing a complex, comprehensive automated manufacturing system is a difficult task—even under the best of circumstances. To be successful, such a project will require smooth and full cooperation among all parties involved: in-house staff, equipment vendors, and, usually, a systems integrator/consultant. Each party should fully understand what the others are capable of doing and have agreed to do. Each company interested in planning an updating program must determine its own mix of inputs from the three parties that best fits its unique circumstances.

14
Caveats and Guidelines

This chapter offers a number of caveats and practical guidelines that should help ensure a successful planning process.

Errors to Be Avoided

Considering the complexity of a comprehensive updating program, the many obstacles it faces, and the significant ramifications for the manufacturing enterprise and its participants, it is not surprising that many updating programs have failed during the relatively short period that they have been attempted. It has been reported that a large percentage, between 30 and 75 percent, of automated manufacturing installations fail at least partly to live up to expectations. These failures are usually due to errors in planning and management, rather than to shortcomings in technology.

The missteps that have been made can be classified under four headings: general planning, specific planning, equipment selection, and execution.

General Planning Missteps

These include:

- The program received insufficient commitment and involvement of top management throughout the planning and implementation process.

- The program lacked adequate long-term, strategic planning (at least 5 to 10 years ahead), and no allowance was made for possible unfavorable developments in the marketplace.

- The program suffered from overoptimistic expectations, insufficient planning, and faulty management of the updating program generally.

- The program was overambitious in scope and timing and too revolutionary for the enterprise and its participants.

- The program concentrated on purely manufacturing functions, did not (sufficiently) include related functions, and/or did not consider the human resource aspects of the updating process.

- The program was driven by the needs of individual functions and departments, rather than by the needs of the enterprise as a whole.

- Undue emphasis was placed on productivity at the expense of increased manufacturing flexibility, one of the principal benefits of automation.

- The underlying strategic plan failed to consider the introduction of new products and product lines that would have become possible with an automated process.

- A plan for the usually lengthy transition period from conventional to automated operations was not prepared.

- Top management of a badly managed enterprise failed to first upgrade the operation with conventional means and improve its labor relations.

- The updating program was initiated as a last resort and could not be supported with adequate financial and other resources.

Specific Planning Missteps

These include:

- Introducing advanced technology for its own sake, rather than as a means for achieving specific business objectives, resulting in added expense and complexity without adding value

- Attempting to integrate all processes by means of comprehensive computer programs (i.e., aiming for computer-integrated manufacturing) in cases where a simpler, noncomputerized integration of the manufacturing installation would be more cost effective

- Automating processes that are more efficiently performed in the conventional manner, i.e., manually or semiautomatically

- Failing to fully exploit the flexibility of an automated installation, e.g., by adding to the number of product variations and by tailoring products to widely differing consumer preferences[1]
- Failing to provide trouble-free communication among all the computerized components of an automated plant, which usually includes equipment and software from a variety of vendors

Equipment Selection Missteps

These include:

- The computers were not rugged to enough to cope with the heat, humidity, electromagnetic radiation, and other conditions that prevail in a typical factory environment.
- The installed automated equipment was too sophisticated for a particular enterprise, plant, or operation.
- The equipment had more features—and was therefore more complex and costly—than was necessary for its intended purpose; this applies especially to equipment that has greater flexibility than is needed or useful.
- Experimental, unproven subsystems were purchased rather than current, off-the-shelf technology. (Any experimentation should be limited to charting new approaches to the integration of proven subsystems and adapting these subsystems to the specific requirements of the new installation.)

Execution Missteps

These include:

- The planning/implementation team was not given sufficient authority and support to accomplish its mission.
- The project leader and members of the planning team were badly selected.

---

[1]U.S. manufacturers—in contrast to Japanese manufacturers—often program their automated installation to turn out large volumes of a few products as if their new installation is only an improved version of their old equipment. They thereby lose out on an important potential benefit of automation.

- Involvement of all the relevant departments and functions in the organization in planning the updating program was not obtained.

- Adequate support from the accounting department for the updating process was not secured. This department, if properly involved and motivated, could make a valuable contribution; if not, it could sabotage the effort.

- Maintenance engineers and equipment operators were not sufficiently involved in the planning and implementation phases, and/or were not encouraged to make needed modifications in the new process after it had been installed.

- There was an overdependence on outside assistance and insufficient participation by in-house staff.

- Planning in the human resources area was inadequate, and the wholehearted support of everyone affected by the updating program was not secured.

- Employees who made a determined effort to adapt to the new process and suggest further innovations were not properly rewarded.

- The existence of restrictive blue-collar work rules was overlooked or inadequately dealt with, thus limiting flexibility in worker assignments, one of the major features of an updated installation.

- Adequate training in operating and maintaining the new installation was not provided.

- The planning team was disbanded at the end of the start-up period, leaving subsequent problems and breakdowns to be dealt with by "green" operators and others who were not involved in the installation of the new process.

Planning Guidelines

Progress in successfully updating a manufacturing enterprise will require fundamental changes in almost all aspects of the organization, including management philosophy, operating practices, and organizational structure, as well as manufacturing processes and equipment.

Top Management Commitment

Since the complete and enthusiastic commitment of top management is a prerequisite for a successful updating program, it follows that no other steps should be taken at any level until and unless such commitment is assured. Also, this commitment must be based on more than just faith in automation or confidence in a certain guru. Therefore, top management must first educate itself in at least a general, nontechnical way in the fundamentals of automating and updating a manufacturing enterprise, and thereby become capable of grasping the importance of properly planning an updating program for their company. This first essential step is dictated by the invasive nature of an updating program, the high cost of implementation, and the considerable risk that this entails.

As part of the indoctrination of top managers in the new technology and procedures, they will have to become more manufacturing oriented than during the past several decades when marketing and finance were their major concerns.

Staff Commitment

Although commitment by top management is the primary need, it is almost equally important that all levels, departments, and functions of the enterprise become fully committed also. All employees must be aware of what is being planned and, hopefully, become enthusiastic about its potential benefit for the company as a whole and—directly or indirectly—for themselves.

Since, in most cases, automation is likely to result in a gradual reduction in the number of employees per given volume of output, the performance of each remaining employee will have an increasing impact on the well-being of the company. This impact is reinforced by the greater sophistication of the equipment and the increased integration of all the functions. Education, training, and the acquisition of multiple skills—sponsored and paid for by the company—will be important tools in encouraging the spread of this needed commitment throughout the organization.

An effort should be made to involve as many employees as early as possible in the planning and implementation process. This will help reduce the normal reaction of many people to resist changes with which they are suddenly confronted.

Steps that can be taken to accomplish this include:

- Making books and articles on the benefits of automation widely available
- Arranging video and slide presentations

- Inviting speakers to discuss the topic
- Encouraging members of various departments to exchange information with their peers concerning their problems and needs and the benefits they expect from automation
- Providing ample opportunity for all staff members to offer input into the planning process whenever it is appropriate

In addition, in order to stimulate worker motivation generally, a determined effort will have to be made to tailor the work to the needs of all employees and to reduce the number of boring tasks and dead-end jobs.

As far as midlevel managers are concerned, although their ranks will gradually be thinned out considerably, there are several reasons why they could play a major role in planning the updating process:

- They are closer to the operations of an enterprise than top managers.
- Many of them are younger than top managers and therefore more likely to be interested in the longer term when automation begins to pay off.
- They are more professionally active and knowledgeable about new technologies and methods, and better able to understand the various intricacies.
- They tend to be less conservative than top managers, yet less impetuous than young professionals.
- They form the communications backbone of the organization.

It is advisable, therefore, for top management to encourage the active participation of middle management in the updating process.

Management Practices

Each company has its own unique set of formal and informal management practices and is characterized by a certain "corporate culture." For an updating process to be successful, the company must almost always change at least some of these practices. Some of the changes that may be required are:

- The decision-making process should become more interactive and collegial, i.e, less dictatorial on the part of the Chief Executive Officer (CEO).

- The company should become more quickly aware of changing trends that affect its operations, e.g., by doing better market research, by keeping better track of technological developments, and by improving the expertise of its staff.

- The organization should become capable of responding more quickly to changing market demands and competitive pressures.

- Product life cycles may have to be shortened, the number of new products increased, new materials considered, and new manufacturing processes introduced as part of the process of becoming a fast-response organization.

- A climate of innovation and teamwork should be established; this change should be initiated by top management, especially in the area of manufacturing automation.

- The role of manufacturing should be given more prominence and emphasis, e.g., by means of promotions and more involvement in the planning process.

- A separate Research and Development (R & D) function should be created to concentrate on manufacturing. In most companies R & D deals only with product development.

- The computer systems of all functional areas of the enterprise should be integrated into a single system.

- Information should become more freely available to all staff members based on need, rather than on the level of authority or reporting relationship.

- Departments should be encouraged to become more cooperative and less competitive.

- Compensation policies must be adjusted to reward all the members of the staff more equitably and should be based on performance and contributions, rather than on the level of authority.

- Management should no longer award itself big bonuses during recessions while cutting wages and laying off workers.

- Layoffs should be avoided or minimized, and superfluous workers retained for other tasks.

- More generally, in order to gain the all-important support of all staff members, special steps should be taken to ensure that no one in the organization will suffer personally as a result of the updating process in terms of income or job security.

- In fact, a special attempt should be made to ensure that almost everyone can expect to *gain* from the implementation of the updating program in terms of compensation, work satisfaction, personal recognition, working conditions, and/or job security.

Education and Training

In addition to securing the commitment of everyone to the updating planning process, there is also a need to educate selected staff members at various levels in some of the technical aspects of automation. There is also a need to train them in the operation of new types of equipment and in working in a totally new organizational structure with new procedures and new relationships. Such education and training should include:

- Surveying presently available automation technologies
- Inspecting existing automated installations and discussing their merits and problems with the engineers who designed and service them
- Attending relevant seminars and taking appropriate courses
- Meeting with vendors and consultants on a preliminary, informal basis

It could be especially helpful to have selected nontechnical top and middle managers visit a few successful automated plants.

All staff members should also be made much more aware of the company's activities and position in the marketplace generally—a prerequisite for gaining their full cooperation and commitment to the company's cause. Bulletins should be issued and meetings held periodically to review the company's goals and accomplishments, the business outlook for the enterprise, the need for updating the company to remain competitive, and specific plans that are under consideration for improving productivity and the company's overall effectiveness.

Reorganization

A successful updating program must incorporate a plan for restructuring the organization and improving its effectiveness. The degree of reorganization that is needed depends on the comprehensiveness of the updating program, e.g., establishing "islands of automation" will require less extensive changes than creating a completely integrated plantwide automated operation.

As indicated previously, all the functions must be better integrated, and the departments must be encouraged to work in close cooperation. This should include the integration of all the information data bases into a single computerized information system. All the information needed to run the enterprise must be entered into the common data base, not just stored in the brains of a few individuals.

Typical changes that may be needed in the structure and functions of the organization are listed below. Not all of these changes are needed in every case—and some may appear to be contradictory:

- Reduce the number of layers of management, delegate more responsibility and authority to lower levels, and widen the span of control of managers, thereby flattening the organizational pyramid and making it leaner
- Reduce the degree of direct supervision, nurture an entrepreneurial attitude, and allow managers to run their unit as a business whenever possible
- Keep the corporate staff small
- Reduce the number of managers and increase the number of knowledgeable specialists
- Establish more flexible work rules, eliminate many functional distinctions and job classifications, and incorporate ancillary and supporting staff functions into line functions
- Adopt a more multidisciplinary approach by encouraging closer cooperation and coordination among product design, manufacturing, purchasing, accounting, and marketing
- Emphasize the needs of the organization as a whole versus those of each department, e.g., by allowing organizational relationships to cut across departmental boundaries, improving communications among departments and functions, and establishing a set of procedures that will promote the development of a more integrated organization
- Make a determined effort to improve the allocation and use of the company's resources, e.g., by increasing the direct customer-contact time of the sales force, reducing the time spent by the marketing staff on administration, and spending more time on effective planning
- Make the manufacturing function more systematic, structured, and explicit (many manufacturing operations still employ a seat-of-the-pants approach)
- Upgrade the materials-handling function so that it can properly perform its essential role as an integrator of the various manufacturing processes and related functions by making it flexible (to accommo-

date different speeds and loads) and modular (so it can be expanded), and by optimizing it (to serve the manufacturing installation as a whole)

One function that has been given short shrift in the past but will gain significantly in importance in an updated, automated enterprise is preventive maintenance. As is clear from the discussion of this topic in Chap. 5, maintenance can no longer remain an organizational afterthought. Maintenance will have to become a major, integral part of the mainstream of the manufacturing enterprise and become a vital ingredient of a company's strategy and competitive strength.

And, finally, it should be noted that the relationships of the updated manufacturing enterprise with its suppliers will have to change considerably. The number of suppliers serving each enterprise will decline, but the bonds with its remaining suppliers will strengthen as follows:

- More suppliers will become captive.
- Subcontracts will be longer term and exclusive.
- Communications with its suppliers will intensify, e.g., by means of online computerized data links.
- Suppliers will be forced to upgrade the quality of their products and to gear their output more closely to the requirements of the manufacturers they serve.

Process Simplification

Although sometimes overlooked, process simplification should be an early key step in any updating program. In fact, in some cases it may turn out that once the process is simplified, no further major improvements are necessary and that extensive automation is not warranted. In other cases, it may lead to the conclusion that automation can be limited to only a few applications within the enterprise.

Process simplification—also known as "rationalization" of the manufacturing process—can sometimes be extremely cost-effective by making changes that cost very little and have a big payoff, and by eliminating or reducing the need for acquiring sophisticated, expensive equipment.

Process simplification starts with a comprehensive, searching analysis of the manufacturing process currently in use. Each operation, process, and procedure is carefully documented. Bottlenecks and problem-prone areas are pinpointed.

Based on this analysis, changes are made that may involve:

- Introducing cellular manufacturing and Group Technology (GT)—not necessarily computerized—and disbanding segregated departments, i.e., replacing a functional setup with a process flow arrangement

- Introducing Just-in-Time (JIT) and eliminating redundant storing of materials, parts, and work in process

- Designing a new master plant layout that will improve the flow of materials and parts

- Improving product manufacturability and facilitating assembly

- Reducing setup time by simplifying each setup through a detailed analysis of each step

- Moving operations and processes closer together and performing tasks only on demand

It should be noted that the computerization of a manufacturing process does not necessarily require the acquisition of automated equipment. It is possible to benefit from computer-directed controls that are applied by human operators to nonautomated equipment.

The planning process needed to convert to such a computerized non-automated operation is similar to that for introducing automation. However, the cost of implementing such a program is much lower, and the benefits could be substantial—although less than the benefits of an automated system installed in an enterprise that is suitable for an automated operation.

The option outlined above is another reason why it is highly desirable to postpone a decision to embark on a comprehensive automation program until after the process-simplification analysis and implementation have been completed. Depending on the size and complexity of the installation, this may take up to 2 years.

Phasing and Follow-up

A key consideration in planning an updating program is the timing of its various constituent parts. Although a few very large companies have been successful in totally updating their enterprise in one swoop, it is generally preferable to phase the implementation in more manageable chunks.

Not only is such a phased approach much more flexible financially, it also facilitates the implementation process by being less failure prone, less disruptive, and more comprehensible to the human mind. This causes less mental stress and reduces the incidence of backlash. It is not surprising, therefore, that incremental automation and retrofitting existing plants have taken place more frequently than the construction of totally new "green field" automated plants.

Lack of capital to create a completely automated installation should never be a reason for not investigating the cost-benefit of updating a manufacturing enterprise. The initial analysis and any subsequent planning are relatively inexpensive and cost-effective.

Implementation of a low-cost conventional manufacturing-process-simplification program outlined in such a plan might be sufficient to save a currently uneconomic enterprise from extinction. If a further step is indicated, a start could be made with partial automation that could prove to be very beneficial without having to get involved with more complete automation and that could be accomplished with a limited outlay of capital funds.

A comprehensive updating program may take 5 or more years of "gut-wrenching" upheaval. Although the new technology may be in place within 18 months, the introduction and taking hold of a new corporate culture and organizational structure will take much longer.

To preserve operational continuity during this period, it is best to tackle one functional area at a time. Start first with new product lines or a new plant, and update the manufacture of existing products at a later time.

The first step should be to establish a sound Manufacturing Resources Planning (MRP-II) system—or improve any existing system. This will require integrating the accounting, order entry, inventory management, costing, and shop floor control functions into a highly accurate centralized data base. This data base is needed to provide the information for analyzing and modifying the company's existing procedures and processes.

In many cases, it is helpful to create several islands of automation, one by one, either as a possibly final stage or as a prelude to integrating such islands into a complete, automated installation. This will facilitate the updating process by making it less revolutionary and more easily absorbable. It also is less risky and provides the option of halting the updating process at an intermediate stage.

Creating islands of automation can be a sound approach, as long as the updating plan makes adequate provision for a possible eventual linkup into an integrated installation that includes an appropriate automated materials-handling system. This means, e.g., establishing uniform standards and protocols for all components, processes, and control systems, and acquiring only compatible equipment.

Closely related to program phasing are the concepts of program monitoring and modification. Updating an enterprise is not a specific goal to be achieved at a particular point in time—at least not with the present state of the art. It is, rather, a continuing, unending, evolving process—rooted in long-range corporate strategy—consisting of successive cycles of planning, designing, and implementing new approaches to manufacturing, usually in fits and starts and with occasional setbacks.

The only goal should be long-term profitability. Automation is only a possible means for helping to accomplish this. The timing and degree of intensiveness will vary for each enterprise and its changing circumstances.

List of Acronyms Used in This Book

ABC	Activity-Based Costing
AEM	Automated Electrified Monorail
AGV	Automated Guided Vehicle
AI	Artificial Intelligence
AS/RS	Automated Storage and Retrieval System
Auto.ID	Automatic Identification
CAD	Computer-Aided Design
CADD	Computer-Aided Drafting and Design
CAE	Computer-Aided Engineering
CAID	Computer-Aided Industrial Design
CAM	Computer-Aided Manufacturing
CAPP	Computer-Aided Process Planning
CE	Concurrent Engineering
CEO	Chief Executive Officer
CFM	Continuous Flow Manufacturing
CIM	Computer-Integrated Manufacturing
CNC	Computer Numerical Controller (or Controlled)
COO	Chief Operating Officer
DCS	Distributed Control System
DFA	Design for Assembly
DFM	Design for Manufacturability
DFMA	Design for Manufacturability and Assembly

DRP	Distribution Requirements Planning
EDI	Electronic Data Interchange
ES	Expert System
FCM	Flexible Cellular Manufacturing
FEA	Finite Element Analysis
FMC	Flexible Manufacturing Cell
FMS	Flexible Manufacturing System
GT	Group Technology
H.R.	Human Resources
HVAC	Heating, Ventilating, and Air Conditioning
I/O	Input/Output
JIT	Just-in-Time
LAN	Local Area Network
MAP	Manufacturing Automation Protocol
MRP	Materials Requirements Planning
MRP-II	Manufacturing Resources Planning
OOPS	Object-Oriented Programming System
OSI	Open Systems Interconnection
P & F	Power and Free
PFA	Production Flow Analysis
PLC	Programmable Logic Controller
PM	Preventive Maintenance
QR	Quick Response
R & D	Research and Development
RFDC	Radio Frequency Data Communication
RFID	Radio Frequency Identification
RISC	Reduced-Instruction-Set Computing
SPC	Statistical Process Control
S/R	Storage/Retrieval
TOP	Technical Office Protocol
TQC	Total Quality Control
UPS	Uninterruptible Power System
WAN	Wide Area Network

Index

About the Author

Peter G. Vanderspek is a management consultant, economist, strategic planner, industrial market researcher, and principal of OBEX, Inc., an international consulting firm. He is a contributor to various trade journals, the recipient of a four-year Thomas J. Watson Fellowship and Scholarship from IBM, and a member of Mensa and the National Association of Business Economists. Dr. Vanderspek holds a Ph.D. in economics.